PHILOSOPHY

IN

100 QUOTES

METRO BOOKS
New York

An Imprint of Sterling Publishing Co., Inc.
1166 Avenue of the Americas
New York, NY 10036

METRO BOOKS and the distinctive Metro Books logo are
registered trademarks of Sterling Publishing Co., Inc.

ISBN 978-1-4351-6781-0

For information about custom editions, special sales, and premium
and corporate purchases, please contact Sterling Special Sales
at 800-805-5489 or specialsales@sterlingpublishing.com.

Manufactured in China

2 4 6 8 10 9 7 5 3 1

sterlingpublishing.com

Design by John Christopher

PHILOSOPHY

IN
100 QUOTES

**GARETH
SOUTHWELL**

METRO BOOKS
New York

INTRODUCTION

Philosophy resists definition. You might say it's concerned with knowledge, but so is science. Is it the search for truth? What about literature, art, or religion? As a subject, it's also very broad and diverse, having evolved over two and a half millennia, and it contains numerous subfields.

Epistemology, or theory of knowledge, asks what knowledge is, where it comes from, and how we can guarantee it. Metaphysics deals with the nature of reality and the fundamental things that constitute and shape it. Moral philosophy focuses on how we should act, how we may justify our actions, and whether a certain behavior or attitude may help us live "the good life." These fundamental concerns may also be applied to other areas: political philosophy looks at such questions as what form of governance—if any—is best, or how we may ensure equality and justice; philosophy of mind explores identity (who and what we are), or how mind relates to body; the philosophy of religion asks if we may prove God's existence, investigates the nature of belief, or how the existence of a deity may be compatible with evil. There is also esthetics (the philosophy of art), feminism, the philosophy of science, broader questions of culture and society (cultural theory), and other areas. So, not only is philosophy's essential nature difficult to define, it may also be applied to anything!

As well as having many applications, it should also be acknowledged that philosophy is perhaps not one tradition, but many. Western philosophy, it's true, began in Ancient Greece, but we cannot deny that China, India, and other cultures, have equally venerable traditions that have evolved their own approaches to the fundamental questions, and so must also be considered "philosophy." And increasingly so, even in the West, many have come to question that philosophy's job is simply to follow dutifully in the footsteps of Plato, Aristotle, and their successors, which has fundamentally changed the nature of philosophy itself.

However, rather than trying to pin down what philosophy *is*, perhaps we should think about what it *does*. Which is what? Fundamentally, it questions. *How do you know that?*, it asks. *Is that the only way of looking at things?* it wonders. Or, if it may politely enquire, *What basis do you have for that assumption?* If you're new to the subject, "Philosophy is questioning" doesn't help much. However, once you discover the types of questions that philosophers have asked, and the answers they've given, you'll hopefully begin to get a feel for what philosophy does.

To help you, this book comprises one hundred philosophical quotations—famous, infamous, controversial, obscure, but all relatively short. There's no duplication—each philosopher is represented only once—and each quote is accompanied by a brief explanation, together with some background about the philosopher and their historical context. Obviously, it's impossible to do justice to each quote and philosopher within such limited space; this book's purpose isn't to tell you everything you need to know, but simply to whet your appetite to find out more.

A journey of a thousand miles begins with a single step.

01

LAOZI

fl. 6th century BC

SOURCE: *Dao De Jing (The Book of the Way and its Virtue)*
DATE: ca. 6th century BC
FIELD: Ethics

Little is known about Laozi, and what is known has an almost mythical quality. It's even possible that he is a composite figure, bringing together the sayings of other unknown philosophers. However, he is traditionally considered the author of the *Dao De Jing — The Book of the Way and Its Virtue* – the 'Way' (*Dao*) referred to being the essential spiritual nature of the universe. This isn't a very satisfying definition, but it's not the translation's fault, for the Dao is in essence inexpressible. As the originating force behind all things, any attempt to name or define it is inevitably unsatisfactory and cannot communicate its true nature.

This ineffability gives Daoism a mystical quality, which, alongside Buddhism, provides an interesting contrast with the Western intellectual tradition arising at the same time. Whereas ancient Greek philosophers pursued intellectual analysis and rational theorising, laying the foundations for natural philosophy (science), their Eastern counterparts took a different path, emphasising self-awareness, humility and harmony with nature. Accordingly, the *Dao De Jing* is unlike most books on ethics in traditional Western philosophy, the closest approach perhaps being stoicism.

This is apparent in the quote, which highlights not a rational path or rule to follow, but an attitude: Pay attention to the here and now, and don't lose sight of the details in pursuit of some larger prize, because the *Dao* is in everything. Then even apparently insignificant things have meaning and consequence. If you stride off, your eyes focused solely on some distant goal, you may trip over your own feet.

Can there
be joy and
laughter

When always
the world
is ablaze?

02

SIDDHARTHA GAUTAMA

fl. 6th century BC

SOURCE: *The Dhammapada*
DATE: ca. 6th century BC
FIELD: Ethics

The *Dhammapada* is a collection of the Buddha's original sayings. Tradition holds that Siddhartha Gautama was a royal prince, born in 6th-century BC Nepal, who gave up his life of privilege to seek spiritual enlightenment. Upon achieving this he earned the accolade "Buddha" ("enlightened one"), and founded a doctrine that is therefore now known as *Buddhism*.

Buddhism advocates a "middle way" between sensual self-indulgence (*hedonism*) and strict self-denial (*asceticism*). Avoiding these two extremes, spiritual peace and insight can be achieved by following an *eightfold path*, which consists in the correct regulation of understanding, emotion, speech, action, livelihood, effort, mindfulness, and concentration. Through practicing Buddhist principles in these areas, the adherent moves closer to enlightenment, which involves liberation (*nirvana*) from the wheel of reincarnation, and which could take thousands of lifetimes to achieve.

The central doctrine of Buddhism is *sunyata* ("emptiness"), which stresses that all things are in truth illusory. We go about our daily lives, our little egos buffeted by pain and pleasure, greedy to acquire this or sad to have lost that, but, in the final analysis, none of this is real: the "I" which you seek so hard to shape, improve, and defend is merely a collection of contradictory and fleeting impressions, whims, and desires, and in truth the cause of all your problems and suffering. For how can we be happy in a world "ablaze" with frustrated desire and pain? It's as if, holding a tiger by the tail, we seek to control it, when the only way to free ourselves is to let go.

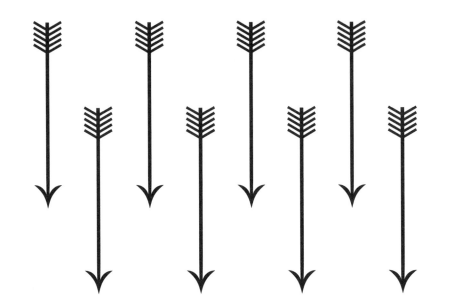

IF YOU KNOW THE ENEMY AND KNOW YOURSELF,
YOU NEED NOT FEAR THE RESULT OF A HUNDRED BATTLES.

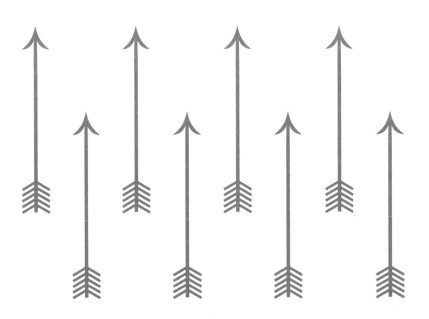

03

SUNZI

544–496 BC

SOURCE: *The Art of War*
DATE: 5th century BC
FIELD: Political philosophy

Sunzi (also known as Sun Tzu) was a Chinese philosopher, contemporary with Confucius and Laozi, whose *Art of War* has become a classic of military strategy and has found modern applications in business and management. As such, it may be said to have a lot in common with both Confucianism and Daoism, though there are also significant differences. For instance, the main purpose of Daoism is to live in humility, in harmony with the *Dao* or "Way," and as such it would seem to shun conflict and worldly ambition. In contrast, although he emphasizes that the best victories are won without fighting, Sunzi seems less concerned with avoiding conflict than with minimizing loss. In this, *The Art of War* is therefore perhaps closer to Machiavelli's *The Prince*, which similarly seeks to advise rulers on the best way to acquire and keep power (we'll look at this later).

That said, the link with Daoism cannot be denied. There is a right time to fight, a best way in which to engage your enemy, and the optimum outcome will always be achieved by being flexible and sensitive to conditions. We can therefore see how Daoist principles may indeed have a military application—we need only look at the philosophy underlying many Eastern martial arts, which often emphasize using your enemy's apparent strength against them, or adapting your strategy to maximize your advantages—he may be bigger and stronger, but you are faster and more elusive. Rather than force, it is therefore in knowledge—not just of one's enemy, but oneself—that victory ultimately lies.

ALL

IS

CHANGE.

HERACLITUS

ca. 540–ca. 470 BC

SOURCE: Quoted in *Refutation of All Heresies* by Hippolytus
DATE: ca. 5th century BC
FIELD: Metaphysics

Heraclitus's philosophy seems as obscure as his life, and there is as much conjecture about who he was as about what he meant by his riddling pronouncements, which exist only in isolated fragments reported at second hand. One of the earliest "pre-Socratic" philosophers (those Greek thinkers who came before Socrates), Heraclitus is chiefly remembered for his contention that everything is in a constant state of change. This is perhaps the meaning of his other well-known assertion that you cannot step into the same river twice, the implication being that, from moment to moment, either you or the river are different. Heraclitus's view is therefore a problem for the notion of *identity*—that is, how something can be said to stay the same through a process of change.

An old illustration of this is the problem known as "Theseus' ship." As the years go by, the ship needs repairing, so eventually all of its wooden planks are replaced with new ones. A modern scientist might make the same point differently: Over time, the cells that make up your body die off and are replaced with new ones; the atoms that make up those cells are in a constant state of flux, interchanging with others in the environment. In this sense, "you" are never the same. So after a number of years, the atoms and cells that make up your body, the planks that make up the ship, will be completely different from the original ones. How then can we say that it's the same ship? Or the same "you"?

There are two sides to every question.

PROTAGORAS

fl. 5th century BC

SOURCE: Quoted in *Lives of the Eminent Philosophers* by Diogenes Laertius
DATE: 5th century BC
FIELD: Epistemology

This seems an uncontroversial, even obvious thing to say. After all, each of us has only a partial view of things, based upon limited experiences and colored by personal values and beliefs. It's therefore common sense that there may be more to any story than any single perspective.

Yet Protagoras was a *sophist*, a type of private tutor common in the ancient Greece of Plato's time. For a fee, a sophist could school you in philosophy, ethics, public speaking, and how to reason and argue. However, more than just a tutor, Protagoras was also a skeptic. He didn't just claim to be able to teach people how to debate, but—as Aristotle describes him as arguing—that "It is equally possible to affirm and to deny anything of anything." More than there being "two sides to every question," Protagoras's position is therefore much more radical: there's no such thing as truth, because an equally persuasive case can be made for any position. Truth, then, is not *objective*, but *subjective*; it doesn't depend on facts or logic, but on how an individual chooses to see things.

Not all sophists were skeptics, but it's easy to see how the philosophical position developed from the educational role. Employed by some rich Athenian to teach them how best to phrase a speech to sway public opinion, or present their case to a jury, truth takes second place. And if truth only gets in the way of a good argument, then what's the point of it anyway?

What you do not want done to yourself, do not do to others.

CONFUCIUS
551-479 BC

SOURCE: *The Analects*
DATE: ca. 470s BC
FIELD: Ethics

For almost two and a half millennia, Confucianism was the dominant philosophy of imperial China. Confucius—a Westernization of Kongfuzi— was a philosopher, teacher, and politician whose doctrines emphasized order, tradition, and moral integrity in both personal and political affairs. His ethical philosophy is embodied in three key principles: *Ren* concerns benevolence, such as empathy for another's suffering or concern for their well-being; *Yi* concerns moral righteousness or justice, such as being truthful and refraining from harming others; and *Li* concerns the duty we owe to authority (parental, governmental, and divine), such as obeying the law or being polite to one's elders.

As such, the quote concerns *Ren*, but primarily *Yi*, and may even be thought of as defining what *Yi* is: doing the right thing *is* simply putting yourself in another's position and considering how you'd want to be treated. This principle is actually common to a number of religious and ethical traditions, and has therefore become known as the Golden Rule, but how should it be applied? If a drug addict were in a position to supply that substance to a fellow addict, then would he be justified in "doing as you would be done by"? Like the Greek philosopher Aristotle, Confucius advocated *virtue ethics*. Often, the right thing to do isn't dictated by some calculation or strict moral code, but is simply what the virtuous *person* would do. Consequently, there could be no such thing as a virtuous addict, because addiction (a lack of rational self-control) is not a virtue.

The things which philosophy attempts to teach by reasoning, poverty forces us to practice.

07

DIOGENES

ca. 400–ca. 325 BC

SOURCE: Quoted in *Anthology* by Johannes Stobaeus
DATE: 4th century BC
FIELD: Ethics

A contemporary of Plato, Diogenes was one of the first "Cynics," a school of Greek philosophy that shunned the trappings of polite society and adopted uncultivated behavior and attitudes in order to emphasize our connection to nature. The word "cynic" comes from the Greek for "dog," possibly a disparaging term used to describe this uncouthness, but which the Cynics seem to have adopted as a badge of honor: Dogs have no false modesty, no shame, will eat and defecate and fornicate when and where they please, but can also be loyal and affectionate. If only *more* people were "dog-like"!

Diogenes himself was famous for living in a sort of earthenware barrel, and he made do with only the bare minimum in terms of possessions—which, aside from the barrel, were the clothes on his back and a simple wooden bowl. In fact, one anecdote relates how, on seeing a boy drink water from cupped hands, he even dispensed with the bowl. His life was therefore a practical illustration of the virtues of simplicity and honesty, and how little human beings actually need to be content. In fact, he argued, it is frequently the added complexity that society brings that causes problems. This point is even easier to appreciate in modern technological cultures, where we are surrounded by pointless luxuries and distractions, spending most of our time worrying about status or cultivating the right online persona. Diogenes would reject many of these things as empty and shallow pursuits. Do you really need them? Do they make you happy?

**BY CONVENTION SWEET IS SWEET, BITTER IS BITTER,
HOT IS HOT, COLD IS COLD, COLOR IS COLOR;
BUT IN TRUTH THERE ARE ONLY ATOMS AND THE VOID.**

08

DEMOCRITUS

ca. 460–ca. 370 BC

SOURCE: Quoted in *Against the Mathematicians* by Sextus Empiricus
DATE: ca. 4th century BC
FIELD: Metaphysics

Democritus was a Greek philosopher roughly contemporary with Socrates. He is often accorded the honor of being the first to advance atomism, although this was probably a view inherited from his teacher Leucippus. While his predecessors debated which element the world ultimately consisted of—earth, water, fire, or air—Democritus argued that the ultimate constituents were in fact tiny, indivisible, indestructible physical entities that were in constant motion, and between which there existed nothing ("the void").

The extent of the debt that modern science owes Democritus is still debated, but perhaps more interesting is the philosophical picture of the universe that we have inherited from him. The material universe is what is ultimately "real," being objective, measurable, and quantifiable, through math and logic; in contrast, sensory experience—taste, sound, color, and so on—is subjective and fleeting, and therefore less "real." Thus, Democritus is one of the first true materialists, arguing that everything can ultimately be reduced to the properties of matter, and his distinction, adopted by later thinkers such as Galileo, Descartes, and Locke, has become a foundation stone for modern scientific enquiry: We should base knowledge not on religious dogma or intuition, but on that which physically exists and can be investigated and tested.

The problem, however, is that this view would itself seem to be an assumption—something which cannot be tested for, but must be taken as a basic premise. Modern problems in the philosophy of mind—specifically, the problem of consciousness (which we'll look at later)—may even suggest that Democritus's particularly narrow conception of "reality" may need revising.

Do I appear to you to have come to a wrong decision, if I devote that time to philosophy, which I otherwise should have spent at the loom?

09

HIPPARCHIA OF MARONEIA
fl. 300 BC

SOURCE: Quoted in *Lives of the Eminent Philosophers* by Diogenes Laërtius
DATE: ca. 4th century BC
FIELD: Feminist philosophy

Originally from Maroniea in Thrace (an area now covering parts of Greece, Bulgaria, and Turkey), Hipparchia later moved to Athens, where she met and married the philosopher Crates. Scant evidence of their ideas has survived (which is not unusual for philosophers of this period), but as with Diogenes, the Cynic philosophy Hipparchia and her husband followed stressed practical example over literary output. What we know of her life and ideas therefore comes not from any texts, but from secondhand stories.

In pursuing Cynic philosophy, Hipparchia is doubly exceptional: Not only was it unusual for a woman to be a philosopher in ancient Greece, but the practices of the Cynics were still regarded by contemporary Greek society as uncouth and even shocking. For a woman to be both was therefore especially remarkable, and it is perhaps difficult to say which of these ancient Greek convention was more offended by.

The quote comes from a debate she had with Theodorus of Cyrene, an infamous atheist. Rather than engage with her points directly, he asked which woman had abandoned her loom, the implication being that she should be embarrassed for neglecting the traditional domestic duties proper to a woman. In response, Hipparchia merely acknowledged that she had abandoned what would be traditionally expected of her sex—but so what? The real question was: Did Theodorus think she was wasting her time? In other words, she was challenging him to find fault with her philosophical arguments, and not with her alleged dereliction of feminine duty.

The unexamined life is not worth living.

10

SOCRATES

469–399 BC

SOURCE: Quoted in *The Apology* by Plato
DATE: 399 BC
FIELD: Ethics

By his own admission, Socrates was a real pain. His favorite activity was to wander Athens looking for anyone who would engage him in debate. Informed by the oracle at Delphi that he was the wisest of all Athenians, but merely because he was the only person who knew that he knew nothing, he took this as a virtue, setting out to question those professing knowledge and wisdom so that they might teach him.

Perhaps this was a rhetorical trick, an attempt to catch his debaters off-guard, but it certainly annoyed enough influential people for Socrates eventually to be hauled before the Assembly on trumped-up charges. Found guilty, he faced a choice: execution, or escape into exile. The latter, he argued, was no life, for wherever he went he was likely to upset people, and therefore face similar problems elsewhere. Why not simply desist from challenging others in this way? However, if he were not free to be himself, to explore the fundamental questions of life, and wherever these led him, then what was the point of living? Surely, such a life would be worthless.

We might wonder why Socrates insists here that philosophy will always get him into trouble. After all, many philosophers are happy to sit and think quietly, without engaging in public controversy or challenging authority. Yet, he seems to imply, this too would be a compromise, for if we do not act on our values, and if we are not prepared to die for them (if necessary), then what sort of values are they?

Doing wrong is worse than suffering wrong.

11

PLATO

427–347 BC

SOURCE: *Gorgias*
DATE: ca. 380 BC
FIELD: Ethics

We may be tempted to disagree with this. Wouldn't we all—selfishly, perhaps—rather wish the opposite? Why is it better to be assaulted than to beat someone? How is it better to be tortured, lied to, or stolen from, than to commit those acts oneself? Plato here criticizes the common view that "Might is right," which sees virtue in terms of dominance and power: The strong prosper at the expense of the weak, and in such a world as we live in, only a fool would choose to suffer for the sake of morality.

The son of an influential Athenian family, Plato was also a follower of Socrates—himself a victim of the abuse of power. In contrast, therefore, Plato argues that the immoral tyrant, who is free to indulge his every whim and desire, is actually *worse off* than the moral person who suffers at his hands. The tyrant is actually *unhappy*, causing harm not only to others, but to *himself*; in contrast, the moral, just person cannot really be harmed. Really? It depends, of course, on your definition of "harm," and perhaps also on religious conviction—yes, you might torture or falsely imprison someone, but, if he is a good person, his *soul* would not be damaged. However, the soul of the immoral tyrant is sick, a disordered mess of warring appetites, meaning that he doesn't actually do what he *wants*, merely what his base desires dictate. As such, we should not envy, but pity him: He is, though he might not admit it, miserable.

Man is
by nature
a political
animal.

12

ARISTOTLE
384–322 BC

SOURCE: *Politics*
DATE: ca. 335 BC
FIELD: Political philosophy

Wearied by corruption, scandal, and controversy, we might be tempted to disagree with Aristotle here: Some might enjoy politics, but surely it is not an *essential* human activity?

"Political" here actually means "relating to the *polis*," referring to the sort of independent city-state that existed in Aristotle's time. A Macedonian, coming to Athens to study under Plato, Aristotle was also well placed to see this most famous city-state with fresh eyes. Yet "city-state" is also misleading, as many *poleis* were neither cities nor states, as we think of them. Firstly, they tended to be small: Aside from exceptions like Athens, Sparta, and Corinth, the average population was around 10,000. Plato suggested an ideal size of around 5,000 households (about 20,000 people), which Aristotle thought too big, merely agreeing with Plato's suggestion that its citizens should be able to recognize one another by sight.

What about "state"? We tend not to think of ourselves as part of the state, but rather as subject to it; it is an independent entity that collects taxes, imposes laws, and administers justice. In contrast, the average citizen of the Greek *polis* was not only expected to engage in political life—by voting (if it were a democracy), or sitting on juries—but to take part in communal and cultural life—attending festivals and rituals, funding public works, putting on plays—and of course, if called upon, to fight in its defense.

Aristotle's point is therefore perhaps better paraphrased as "Humans are by nature social beings," whose mutual happiness and fulfillment requires being part of a community.

Human nature seems to me to provide a standard of law and justice both for the home and for the city.

13

AESARA
ca. 4th to 3rd century BC

SOURCE: *On Human Nature*
DATE: ca. 4TH to 3RD century BC
FIELD: Political philosophy

Historically, philosophy seems to have been as male-dominated as most other professions, and from the earliest Greeks until relatively recently there have been few women philosophers. One of the earliest female philosophers in the Western tradition was Aesara of Lucania (an area of what is now southern Italy), a fragment of whose sole surviving work seems to show the influence of Plato. Like him, Aesara sees the true basis of morality, law, and justice as lying in human nature itself. In the *Republic*, Plato argued for just such a view, dividing his ideal state into three social classes—rulers, auxiliaries (soldiers, ministers), and producers (farmers, craftsmen, the common people)—corresponding to the three aspects of the soul—reason, "spirit" (emotion), and desire. It is therefore the role of reason (embodied in the rulers, or "philosopher kings") to govern the person (the state), keeping in check the potentially unruly desires (the general populace). Justice therefore consists in the proper relation of these parts, both in the person and in society at large.

While agreeing with this general division and approach, it's interesting to note that Aesara's view differs as to the respective nature of these parts and how they interact. Whereas Plato emphasizes the need for top-down discipline and rational control, Aesara sees each aspect as working together harmoniously and complementing their differences and respective strengths and weaknesses. While Plato saw desire as a many-headed and dangerous beast that must be vigorously kept in check, Aesara emphasized the positive contribution that desire makes to love, family, and friendship.

NEVER HAS A MAN WHO HAS BENT HIMSELF BEEN ABLE TO MAKE OTHERS STRAIGHT.

14

MENGZI

ca. 371–ca. 289 BC

SOURCE: *The Mengzi*
DATE: ca. 4th/3rd century BC
FIELD: Ethics

Mengzi, also known by the Westernized name of Mencius, was a Chinese philosopher who lived some two centuries after Confucius, and whose work was an interpretation and development of Confucianism. Like the philosopher who inspired him, Mengzi emphasized the importance of adopting the correct moral attitude and behavior, regardless of the situation.

Mengzi was once asked why he did not involve himself with political figures and those in power. Surely, by doing so, he could exert greater influence, even perhaps influence the fate of a whole nation. In reply, Mengzi cited the example of a forester who, when commanded by his duke to assist him on the hunt, refused to leave his regular duties. In doing so, the forester risked the duke's wrath, punishment, and even death.

Mengzi's point here is that we are often faced with situations where a particular course of action tempts us away from our moral duty or true sense of what is right. In such circumstances, we may be influenced by fear, ambition, or some other non-rational motive, but even if the objective seems very rational and noble—such as seeking the favor of rulers in order to help better govern the state—if it draws the person away from his correct path of conduct, then it is the wrong choice. Mengzi recognized that, for someone such as himself, this principle was even more important, for how can a teacher and philosopher advise and guide others when he himself does not follow what he knows to be right?

How do I know that in hating death we are not like people who got lost in early childhood and do not know the way home?

15

ZHUANGZI
369–298 BC

SOURCE: *The Zhuangzi*
DATE: ca. 4th to 2nd centuries BC
FIELD: Epistemology

Zhuangzi was a Chinese Daoist philosopher whose book of the same name (which may also include later, anonymous contributions) is considered one of the central texts of Daoism. In contrast to his contemporaries, Zhuangzi rejected Confucianism, preferring the teachings of Laozi. *The Zhuangzi* therefore portrays the ideal behavior and attitudes of the perfect Daoist sage, whose wisdom allows him to live free of the anxieties and stresses common to most ordinary people.

Taking one of these anxieties—our fear of death—the quote questions what we think we know about it. We assume that, in dying, we exchange a familiar here and now for an uncertain and frightening future state, be that annihilation or some form of postmortem existence. However, Zhuangzi points out that since we really know nothing of death, there is no ground for certainty either way. In fact, given our lack of knowledge in general, it's as likely that what we think of as "life" is itself the strange, confusing state, and death is a return home.

The Zhuangzi often uses skepticism to blur and disrupt our common conceptions. Another famous example has the sage waking from the dream of being a butterfly; but has he really awoken, or is he now only a butterfly dreaming he is Zhuangzi? The point with both these examples is that the fear and uncertainty that disrupt our natural state of tranquillity are often baseless. Why worry about what is ultimately real, what awaits us after death, or other insoluble puzzles? As with Buddhism, it's not through answering but relinquishing such fruitless questions that we achieve happiness.

Of all the means which are procured by wisdom to ensure happiness throughout the whole of life, by far the most important is the acquisition of friends.

EPICURUS
341–270 BC

SOURCE: *Principal Doctrines*
DATE: ca. 3rd century BC
FIELD: Ethics

In modern usage, "epicure" describes someone who values the finer things of life: a connoisseur of pleasure, especially food and wine. However, the Greek philosopher Epicurus, from whom we get the word, was more restrained in his tastes, arguing that pleasure is the chief good (*hedonism*). By this he meant not that we should blindly pursue pleasure for its own sake, but rather cultivate those specific pleasures that most avoid physical and mental pain, helping to develop tranquillity of both body and mind. Therefore, a true epicurean is more likely found enjoying a homely, freshly prepared meal of simple, quality ingredients than a sophisticated, avant-garde culinary experiment served at some expensive, high-end restaurant.

Higher than sensual pleasure was that of friendship. Bodily pleasures are linked to desire, which is itself a form of pain: we hunger or thirst, ache with lust, are bored or guilty from overindulgence. In contrast, true friendship asks nothing, but supplies companionship and conversation, helping ease the anxiety, fear, and loneliness all humans face. As such, it is one of the highest and purest pleasures we can feel.

Is Epicurus being consistent here? As other philosophers have pointed out, Epicurus's ethical hedonism, which sees morality in terms of pleasure, seems to require that he defines the value of friendship in terms of selfish gratification. Is that true friendship, however? Alternatively, if he values friendship for its own sake—perhaps friendship is about more than personal pleasure—he risks being philosophically inconsistent. So which is he: a bad friend, or a bad philosopher?

FOR
LAWS
ARE
SILENT
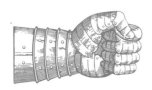 
WHEN
ARMS
ARE
RAISED.

17

CICERO
106–43 BC

SOURCE: *Pro Milone*
DATE: 52 BC
FIELD: Political philosophy

Marcus Tullius Cicero was a Roman politician, lawyer, orator, and philosopher. The quote is drawn from a speech he made on behalf of his friend, Titus Annius Milo, who had been accused of murdering a political adversary. Cicero's defense consisted in arguing that the laws that govern our behavior in ordinary situations are different to those that should apply in circumstances of war and conflict. Since Milo's actions were a response to being physically attacked, they should therefore not be considered a criminal act of murder, but as proceeding from his own legitimate need to protect himself.

Cicero was among the first philosophers to attempt to establish principles for what is termed "just war," and his argument here is perhaps best understood in that context. Since war necessarily involves killing, assault, destruction of property, and other things we would normally condemn, there need to be good reasons for justifying those acts. As his argument regarding Milo suggests, one justification for war is self-defense; if our country is attacked, we may respond with equal force. However, the response should be proportionate; a border skirmish might not warrant a full-scale invasion. War should also be conducted in the proper way: Civilians should not be targeted, and we should also treat prisoners humanely. Additionally, of course, war should only be conducted by the proper authority, and come as a last resort; hostilities could only commence once the offending party had been given the opportunity to apologize or make amends. In which case, though war might involve different laws, it should not silence the law altogether.

When a man does not know what harbor he is making for, no wind is the right wind.

SENECA THE YOUNGER
4 BC to 65 AD

SOURCE: *Moral Letters to Lucilius*, "Letter LXXI: On the Supreme Good"
DATE: ca. 65 AD
FIELD: Ethics

Lucius Annaeus Seneca, or Seneca the Younger, as he is most commonly known (to distinguish him from his father, who was also a writer), was a Roman statesman and dramatist. He followed the Stoic philosophy, first set out by Zeno of Citium, which counseled a life of simplicity lived in accordance with nature, and a calm acceptance of those things that are beyond our control. As such, a stoic attempted to restrain desires, overcoming sensual temptation or the negative promptings of fear or pain, and to maintain a state of tranquillity of mind in the face of physical danger or emotional turmoil.

The quote illustrates the importance of this state of equanimity through the metaphor of a sea journey. Like the unpredictable wind and sea, our emotions and desires may buffet our reason one way or another, driving us blindly from problem to problem, even threatening our very existence. However, the tranquil mind will be impervious to such disruptions. Realizing that there are many things that are beyond our control, and that pleasure and pain are fleeting impressions, we should focus on what we want to achieve—not driven by emotion or desire, fear or pain, but directing our will in line with the natural order of things. Those things we can change, we should; those we can't, we should accept. Contentment lies not in the satisfaction of some physical want or emotional need, but in the cultivation of an indifference to whatever fate may throw in our path.

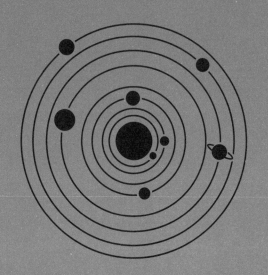

THAT WHICH
IS BELOW
CORRESPONDS
TO THAT WHICH
IS ABOVE,

AND THAT
WHICH IS ABOVE
CORRESPONDS
TO THAT WHICH
IS BELOW.

HERMES TRISMEGISTUS
fl. between 1st and 3rd century AD

SOURCE: *The Emerald Tablet*
DATE: Between 1st and 3rd centuries AD
FIELD: Metaphysics

The quote comes from the *Hermetica*, a collection of texts—once thought to predate Christianity by a thousand years—that deals with such subjects as alchemy, astrology, magic, spiritual enlightenment, and humanity's nature and place in the universe. Their alleged author, "Thrice-Great Hermes," was thought to be a contemporary of the Jewish prophet Moses, and considered "thrice-great" in that he possessed at once the wisdom of a priest, philosopher, and king.

This claim to antiquity was later disproven, and it is now mostly held that the texts date from between the 1st and 3rd centuries AD, though they may still perhaps be taken as setting down older lost texts or oral traditions. Whatever the case, there is no denying the texts' enormous influence upon the Renaissance, as illustrated by the now widely familiar notion of "as above, so below." This may be interpreted in various ways, but perhaps its most common application is in the idea that a human being is made in God's image and therefore represents in miniature (the *microcosm*) the divinely ordained order of the universe itself (the *macrocosm*). This correspondence might also play out at other levels: the monarch ruled on earth as God ruled in heaven; the stars and planets determined aspects of human affairs and character; the king ruled his subjects as a person's reason guided and controlled their emotions and desires (interestingly, an idea that we also find in Plato's *Republic*). That being so, the correspondence between levels of being—psychological, political, astrological—was itself a sign of God's handiwork.

If any be unhappy,
let him remember that
he is unhappy by reason
of himself alone.

20

EPICTETUS
55–135 AD

SOURCE: Quoted in *Discourses of Epictetus* by Arrian of Nicomedia
DATE: ca. 108
FIELD: Ethics

Epictetus was another Stoic, but one whose philosophical forbearance developed not through a life of politics and literary pursuit, but as a slave. Born into enforced servitude in Phrygia (now part of Turkey), it's easy to see how Stoicism appealed to him, with its emphasis on acceptance of our essential powerlessness in the hands of fate. However, even when he eventually achieved his freedom, and despite later acquiring considerable fame for his philosophy and public speaking, Epictetus continued to live a life of great simplicity.

The quote emphasizes that happiness is up to us—not in the sense that we may better our circumstances, but rather that we must change our attitude to them. This isn't to say that we should *never* seek change, nor that we must try to "look on the bright side," but rather that we should seek to understand what is within our power to alter. So, while Epictetus thought that we might change our mental habits, train our emotional responses, and curtail our desires, we can not always affect external events—even our own bodies are subject to disease and accident. Better, then, to focus on what could be changed.

For example, you are upset to hear that a friend has disparaged you. Should you confront them? Shun them? Epictetus would say that what others think of you is not yours to decide. Even the best person may be slandered. The opinions of others, like the events of the world, are "external" to us, beyond our control. Only our feelings about these opinions are ours to change.

WHATEVER
HAPPENS
AT ALL
HAPPENS AS
IT SHOULD.

21

MARCUS AURELIUS
121–180

SOURCE: *Meditations*
DATE: ca. 170–180
FIELD: Ethics

Stoicism's breadth of appeal is revealed in the fact that its adherents included not just slaves and dramatists, but even emperors. Roman Emperor Marcus Aurelius may perhaps lay claim to being the closest embodiment of Plato's ideal of the philosopher king, and his *Meditations* sets down his personal struggle to employ the principles of Stoicism both in his personal and public life.

The quote, as you will by now recognize, stresses the importance of the Stoic's belief in fate; but what did they mean by this? A ruler daily makes decisions that affect thousands. He cannot always simply let events unfold. Rather, then, "fate" is what happens *despite* our best efforts.

However, if everything "happens as it should," then doesn't that *include* our actions? Do Stoics therefore deny freedom of the will? The possibility that even our thoughts and emotions may be physically predetermined wouldn't fully flower until the advent of modern science. The Stoics merely thought that mind, and therefore will, emotion, and desire, were subject to rational control, whereas the physical world (including the body) was not.

Yet even if this is so, how do we know when to sit back or push forward? What determines the right course of action? As already noted, Stoics believed in a natural order to things, which Aurelius calls a *logos*, a rational principle that governs the world. Whether or not this is God, its rational nature provided a path that the calm-minded student of events could identify and follow.

ALTHOUGH YOU MAY SPEND YOUR LIFE KILLING, YOU WILL NOT EXHAUST ALL YOUR FOES. BUT IF YOU QUELL YOUR OWN ANGER, YOUR REAL ENEMY WILL BE SLAIN.

22

NAGARJUNA
fl. 1st–2nd century

SOURCE: *The Staff of Wisdom*
DATE: ca. 2nd century
FIELD: Ethics

Not much is known of Nagarjuna, although it is thought that he was born a Hindu in southern India, before eventually turning to Buddhism.

For Nagarjuna, all phenomena were ultimately empty, inasmuch as everything that we experience is in fact a mental creation. This is not to say that the world does not really exist—Nagarjuna is not making a skeptical point about the nature of existence (that it is all a dream, perhaps)—but to point out that pain or pleasure, sensation or desire, are not things in themselves, but fleeting shadows cast by the movement of our own consciousness.

This notion of emptiness (*sunyata*) is central to Nagarjuna's teaching, and is therefore also key to understanding the quotation. In war and other forms of conflict, many cultures consider it legitimate to take the life of an enemy. In such circumstances, anger may be considered a necessary, even a noble thing. However, the frame of mind which sees people in terms of friends and foes, victories and defeats, is itself an unsettled one, and arguably one that can never find contentment. The only victory is over anger itself, which to conquer requires psychologically dismantling the concepts and categories that give rise to it.

How can this be achieved? Someone does something which offends your pride, but everything involved—the behavior, the offence you feel, the "self" whose pride is wounded by it—has no real basis other than your belief that these things are "real." Let that go, and anger goes with it.

We are too weak by unaided **reason** to find out truth.

23

ST. AUGUSTINE OF HIPPO
354–430

SOURCE: *Confessions*
DATE: 397–400
FIELD: Philosophy of religion

Augustine was the Christian bishop of Hippo, a Roman city in what is now Algeria, North Africa. As a young man, although interested in religious matters, he was also somewhat of a libertine; aware of this contradiction, he famously called on God to make him chaste and restrained—but not just yet.

Drawn first to Manicheanism (a Persian form of Gnosticism that saw the universe as a battleground for the forces of light and darkness), then later to neo-Platonism (a doctrine that from the 3rd century AD onward developed upon the teachings of Plato), only his eventual discovery of Christianity allowed Augustine to finally trade his sinful love of carnal pleasure for a virtuous life.

Why had it taken so long? Why had Christianity succeeded where other faiths, and the rational teachings of neo-Platonic philosophers, had both failed? Augustine argued that it was because faith is not something that we can decide upon, a conclusion to be arrived at purely by rational argument, but something that requires God's intervention—His *grace*. The reason for this is that all human faculties had been tainted by the Fall (the temptation of Adam and Eve and their expulsion from the Garden of Eden). Furthermore, the rational faculties are closely tied to the sin of pride and self-reliance—our cleverness convinces us that we don't need God. Such an attitude can never lead to faith, and belief itself is more than merely signing up to a set of dogmas. Rather, what's needed is radical *self-transformation*, which requires humility, sincerity, but most of all, divine assistance.

24

ST. ANSELM
1033–1109

SOURCE: *Proslogion, Discourse on the Existence of God*
DATE: 1077–1078
FIELD: Philosophy of religion

The *ontological* argument has tangled philosophers' minds for centuries. Ontology is the part of philosophy that considers being or existence—what types of things exist, what is the nature of their existence, and so forth. Here, Anselm, an Italian-born archbishop and theologian, uses this approach to argue for the existence of God.

We may think of God as a being so powerful, knowledgeable, and so on, that it is impossible to conceive of anything greater—for, if we *could*, then surely *that* being would be God. So, God is a being than which none greater can be conceived, but does that being actually exist? Well, if He *didn't* exist, then He would only exist in the mind. Yet we could then conceive of a *greater* being— that is, one that existed not only in the mind, as an idea, but in reality also. So, in conceiving of the greatest being (God), we therefore would seem to conceive of one that necessarily exists. So, simply by having the idea, we can know that God exists.

The reasoning is ingenious and elegant, but also, like some magic trick, leaves us uneasy, doubting our own judgment. Has Anselm proven the existence of God, or is it some logical sleight of hand? A famous objection, by the monk Gaunilo of Marmoutier, pinpoints this unease. Imagine, he says, the perfect island, none greater than which can be conceived. Does that mean it exists? Most would say not—it's just an ideal. However, if we feel unsure in granting the perfect island existence, then why not God?

It seems that no word can be used literally of God.

ST. THOMAS AQUINAS
ca. 1225–1274

SOURCE: *Summa Theologica*
DATE: 1265–74
FIELD: Philosophy of religion

According to Christian scripture and tradition, God's qualities surpass anything we can experience: As good, or powerful, or wise as we may be, what human being could even come near to God? Then isn't God beyond human comprehension, an external, suprahuman force that we can never directly relate to?

In addressing this problem, the Italian priest and theologian Thomas Aquinas argued that religious language is neither *univocal* (literally true) nor *equivocal* (having separate senses for God and humans), but *analogical* (metaphorical). This third way therefore sees statements about God as making a sort of comparison or analogy. To say "God is good" is not true in the same literal sense as when I say "I am good"; nor does it have a completely separate and unrelated sense, for then there would be no way for us to understand God's goodness, and no connection of his moral commands to our behavior. Rather, religious language suggests an *analogy* or *relationship* between my goodness and that of God.

This analogy works in two ways: by *proportion* and *attribution*. God's "goodness," *in proportion* to his superior being, is different (but related) to mine, just as a person's goodness is different (but related) to that of a "good" dog. Furthermore, my goodness *is attributed to* me because my actions share in God's attribute of goodness (my goodness depends on Him), whereas God Himself simply *is* good—just as a hand may be warmed by a fire, but the fire is hot by its own nature. Thus, we may know God through analogy, despite the gulf in being.

PLURALITY MUST NEVER BE POSITED WITHOUT NECESSITY

PLURALITY MUST NEVER BE POSITED WITHOUT NECESSITY

PLURALITY MUST NEVER BE POSITED WITHOUT NECESSITY

PLURALITY MUST NEVER BE POSITED WITHOUT NECESSITY

PLURALITY MUST NEVER BE POSITED WITHOUT NECESSITY

PLURALITY MUST NEVER BE POSITED WITHOUT NECESSITY

PLURALITY MUST NEVER BE POSITED WITHOUT NECESSITY

PLURALITY MUST NEVER BE POSITED WITHOUT NECESSITY

PLURALITY MUST NEVER BE POSITED WITHOUT NECESSITY

PLURALITY MUST NEVER BE POSITED WITHOUT NECESSITY

PLURALITY MUST NEVER BE POSITED WITHOUT NECESSITY

PLURALITY MUST NEVER BE POSITED WITHOUT NECESSITY

PLURALITY MUST NEVER BE POSITED WITHOUT NECESSITY

PLURALITY MUST NEVER BE POSITED WITHOUT NECESSITY

PLURALITY MUST NEVER BE POSITED WITHOUT NECESSITY

PLURALITY MUST NEVER BE POSITED WITHOUT NECESSITY

PLURALITY MUST NEVER BE POSITED WITHOUT NECESSITY

PLURALITY MUST NEVER BE POSITED WITHOUT NECESSITY

PLURALITY MUST NEVER BE POSITED WITHOUT NECESSITY

WILLIAM OF OCKHAM
1285-1349

SOURCE: *Commentary on the Sentences of Peter Lombard*
DATE: 1317–1318
FIELD: Metaphysics

This pithy little dictum is known as "Ockham's razor," named for its deviser, William of Ockham, an English Franciscan friar. It's also known as the *principle of parsimony*: If you can do without it, then you don't need it. This applies to explanations, especially in relation to science and metaphysics. Faced with two possible accounts of why something happens, we should favor the simpler one (more or less).

An example of the application of this principle can be found in biology. It once was accepted wisdom that living beings require some vital essence or spirit to make them alive (a view known as *vitalism*). However, others began to question this, arguing that we can account for the functioning of living creatures in a *mechanistic* way—that is, in terms of an organism's machine-like interaction of parts. If we can do so successfully, without leaving anything unexplained, need we also assume a "vital spirit"?

This approach has also taken root in modern philosophy of mind. If we can explain the mind simply through the workings of the physical brain, then why assume the existence of a soul or spirit? Except that here, there's a problem: Human beings are not only living, biological entities, but conscious and sentient—we are *aware*, we *think* and *feel*. Can the materialist, mechanistic view of the mind account for this? Some argue not, and that, at the very least, our notions of matter need revising. For, though it may be simpler to ignore such problems, doing so does not bring us closer to truth.

My own wish is
to be a citizen of
the world, to be a
fellow-citizen to
all men.

27

ERASMUS
1469–1536

SOURCE: Letter to Huldrych Zwingli
DATE: September 3, 1522
FIELD: Political philosophy

Desiderius Erasmus was a Dutch scholar and theologian whose writings advanced a form of Christian *humanism*. The term comes from the rekindling of interest in Greek and Roman texts during the Renaissance, the study of which became known as the "humanities" (those "liberal arts"—such as philosophy, literature, and history—that tended to deal with human affairs as opposed to religious ones). This influenced a cultural shift away from a faith-based approach to study toward a more rational attitude.

These days, the term "humanism" often contrasts something with its religious counterpart—a humanist funeral, for example, as opposed to one conducted by a minister of religion. However, as Erasmus illustrates, the two were not always distinct, and his Christian humanism displays the sort of liberal and enlightened interpretation of religious doctrine (his "middle way") that moved away from literal fundamentalism.

One consequence of this attitude is illustrated in the quote. While never denying his Dutch heritage, Erasmus considered the spiritual and natural ties that unite people to be more important. It is in this sense, then, that we are all "citizens of the world," because (in medieval Europe, at least) we are all united through God, and through our common humanity. A scholar might also share in the intellectual community, where a German and a Spaniard, neither knowing each other's language, might nonetheless converse in the *lingua franca* of scholarship (Latin or Greek). And yet, ironically, it was also perhaps his "middle way"—his refusal to identify himself with one doctrine, camp, or national cause—that also made him an outsider.

FOR ALTHOUGH THE ACT CONDEMNS THE DOER, THE END MAY JUSTIFY HIM.

28

NICCOLÒ MACHIAVELLI

1469–1527

SOURCE: *Discourses on Livy*
DATE: 1531
FIELD: Political philosophy

For centuries, Machiavelli has been a dirty word, and "Machiavellian" a term of extreme disapproval, synonymous with ruthless cunning and moral bankruptcy. Now, we're perhaps less scandalized by his views than were his contemporaries—being more resigned, perhaps, to the deceit and hypocrisy of politicians—but his candor can still be shocking.

A diplomat and statesman in Renaissance Florence, Machiavelli witnessed first-hand the unflinching methods employed by the notorious Borgia family, coming to realize in his infamous work of political philosophy, *The Prince*, that, admirable and noble as it would be for rulers to employ Christian values, in practice this just wouldn't work. Nice guys finish last, and naive trust in the goodness of others would ensure a short rule indeed. Machiavelli therefore recognized that to maintain an orderly, just society it was occasionally necessary for a ruler to get his hands dirty. For instance, it might be necessary to lie, torture, and even perhaps kill, in order to ensure that the ruler's authority and power were not undermined. In other words, as the quote suggests, there may be occasions where, paradoxically, doing good means being bad, where the end justifies the means.

We're perhaps not so shocked by this now. Modern governments are frequently caught being "economical with the truth," contravening civil rights, spying, stealing, and employing other illegal methods. What's still shocking, however, is that Machiavelli wouldn't consider such things a sign of corruption, but of necessity: All government involves immorality; the best simply get away with it.

Nothing is so
firmly believed, as
what we least know.

29

MICHEL DE MONTAIGNE
1533-1592

SOURCE: *Essays*
DATE: 1588
FIELD: Epistemology

Surely, we reserve our strongest conviction for that which we know *most* about? Montaigne's point is that, while in theory our lack of knowledge should caution restraint, the greater mystery involved gives us greater license to believe what we want. And for this reason, people will assert and believe any manner of thing in religious matters that they would not entertain in human affairs.

Michel de Montaigne was a French philosopher who is now best known for his *Essays*, a collection of short pieces on a wide range of subjects, from virtue to thumbs, from fear to cannibalism. The key theme is a general skepticism concerning the extent and certainty of human knowledge, which Montaigne uses to argue that, since there seems to be very little about which we can be absolutely certain, then we are often better off suspending judgment.

Like Erasmus before him, Montaigne was a humanist, often approaching moral questions in human, psychological terms, not theological ones. With Descartes (discussed later), whom he was to influence, he shared a belief in rational caution over blind faith. This is not to say that Montaigne was atheistic, or perhaps even agnostic, in religious matters—he certainly seems to have taken his own faith seriously. However, his skepticism did lead him to advocate a degree of tolerance. For, faced with the unknowable will of God, who are we to claim that our actions or practices are divinely favored, and those of others condemned? History supplies enough examples of the unjust thriving while the just suffer. Who, then, are we to judge? Is *all* knowledge empowering? The Internet has provided an unprecedented means for the sharing of information, but as we sift through our social media feeds, check our emails, or casually surf the web, are we really any more enlightened than previous generations?

INFORMATION

INFORMATION

KNOWLEDGE

INFORMATION

INFORMATION

INFORMATION

INFORMATION

ITSELF IS POWER

30

FRANCIS BACON
1561-1626

SOURCE: "Of Heresies" in *Sacred Meditations*
DATE: 1597
FIELD: Philosophy of science

Information isn't knowledge. Some may be useless, or at least seem to provide no practical benefit. Yet even useful information, while it sits there unanalyzed, does not by its mere existence in our memory add to our store of what we know. Before we can say we know something, we must process or utilize this information in some way.

Francis Bacon, an English Elizabethan lawyer, statesman, and philosopher, is sometimes credited with providing the philosophical basis for the scientific revolution. For a millennium, European thought had been dominated by the uneasy marriage of Christian theology and the philosophy of Aristotle, creating a static worldview—*Scholasticism*—that it could be heretical, even dangerous to question. This, Bacon argued, had held back science and philosophy, producing untested assumptions as unquestioned as the dogmas of faith, where "knowledge" might be amassed irrespective of its application, and fruitless controversies thrived. As fascinating as it might be to consider whether there were toilets in heaven—even *if* we could find out—how much would this advance the human condition? Rather, we should favor questions that were both answerable and testable, hence the emphasis on evidence and experiment.

Of course, Bacon is mainly concerned with "natural philosophy" (science), but we may also apply his insight more generally: Unless we profit *in some sense* from the information we gather, what's the point of it?

The mother of right—that is, of natural law—is human nature.

31

HUGO GROTIUS
1583–1645

SOURCE: *On the Law of War and Peace*
DATE: 1625
FIELD: Political philosophy

Laws differ from country to country, and often change over time. Does that mean, then, that they are merely conventions with no absolute basis? This would seem to be problematic, especially in terms of international relations, or concerning those issues that affect us all—for instance, environmental law and the dangers of climate change.

The idea that laws are merely human constructions is known as *legal positivism*, and has been advanced by such philosophers as Jeremy Bentham, who also opposed the idea of "natural rights." What determines law is not some objective, independent standard to which we can appeal (God, or human nature), but the evolution of social customs, institutions and attitudes. A law may therefore seem outdated or unjust, but still be the law.

Legal positivism is a response to *natural law* theory, which is the position advanced in the quotation by the Dutch jurist and legal theorist Hugo Grotius. Rather than consider law a matter of mere convention, natural law proposes that what is legal is determined by certain facts about human nature and the world, which can be directly perceived by reason. It is in this spirit that the US Constitution considers the various rights it enshrines to be "self-evident." Grotius even went as far as to argue that such truths did not depend on God, but were inherent in human nature itself—having created human nature, even God could not subvert it.

Returning to international relations, what did it mean when two countries' laws differed? Obviously, Grotius would say, according to natural law, one—or both—must be wrong.

I think, therefore I am

32

RENÉ DESCARTES
1596–1650

SOURCE: *Meditations on First Philosophy*
DATE: 1641
FIELD: Epistemology

It is an old, well-known joke—well known among philosophy students, anyway—Descartes walks into a bar and orders a drink. "Another?" asks the barman. "I think not," Descartes replies, and promptly vanishes out of existence.

French philosopher René Descartes was a scientist and mathematician, and is often considered the father of modern philosophy. The joke plays on a certain interpretation of his most famous pronouncement, "I think, therefore I am," implying that if we were to stop thinking, at any time, then we would also cease to exist. However, this isn't what Descartes meant.

In his *Meditations*, Descartes asks whether there's anything we can know beyond doubt. Since most information comes through our senses, and it's not unknown for our eyes and ears to be wrong, why trust them at all? He also notes that we may sometimes dream that we are awake; who is to say, then, that we are not dreaming now? Yet even if our senses deceive us, and the "real" world is but a dream, surely rational truths, such as those of logic and mathematics, won't let us down? Surely, I still know that "2 + 2 = 4"? However, doesn't this assume that reason itself is trustworthy? What if some all-powerful, malignant force existed—some "malignant demon," as Descartes calls it—that could fool me regarding the trustworthiness of such apparent certainties?

Descartes's solution was that, even if we *could* doubt such "certainties," we could not be fooled as to our very existence, because in order to doubt, we must think; and to think, we must exist.

Words are wise men's counters, they do but reckon by them; but they are the money of fools.

33

THOMAS HOBBES
1588–1679

SOURCE: *Leviathan*
DATE: 1651
FIELD: Philosophy of language

Does it matter what we call things? If, as Shakespeare puts it, "A rose by any other name would smell as sweet," then aren't words arbitrary labels that we can swap around as we please? This is not such an issue with proper names: Elizabeth may be "Liz" or 'Beth," or some other nickname, but she is still the same person. The same applies to the Eiffel Tower or the Grand Canyon. If anyone is unsure what we mean, we can still point to the thing itself.

Where it gets problematic, however, is in relation to general and abstract terms—"tree" or "dog," "beauty" or "justice." Here, we cannot point to one thing—Liz or the Eiffel Tower—because a single term covers many different instances. Yet how then do we know that the same term—"justice," for example—picks out the same qualities in each case?

One answer, favored by Plato and other *rationalist* philosophers, is *realism*: that the idea of justice, for example, is in some sense *real*, existing independently from each individual instance it applies to. However, while rationalism emphasizes abstract ideas, English philosopher Thomas Hobbes adopts an empiricist approach, which sees experience as playing the central role. His view is known as nominalism: What trees have in common is not that they share some resemblance to the ideal notion of a tree, but that they share similarities with other things we call trees. And so, we should not get too hung up on words. Words can change; what is important are the features they pick out.

**THE HEART HAS ITS REASONS,
WHICH REASON DOES NOT KNOW.**

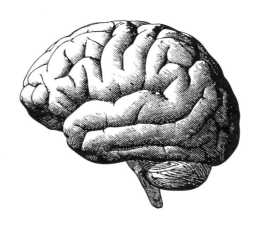

34

BLAISE PASCAL
1623–1662

SOURCE: *Pensées*
DATE: 1670
FIELD: Philosophy of religion

French philosopher Blaise Pascal was a man torn in two directions, so he felt, by the contrary impulses of religious conviction and a fascination with science and philosophy. Though a precociously talented mathematician, a religious experience would later cause him to doubt the value of all rational knowledge. In line with St. Augustine, Pascal considered that human reason was insufficient for moral goodness, poisoned by the fruit of the tree of knowledge in Eden. As such, it could not even be used to prove God's existence.

The closest Pascal came to such a proof was his celebrated "wager": If we consider the potential rewards and punishments of religious belief and disbelief, and weigh up the consequences of both, then, he argued, belief is by far the best option. Admittedly, if you believe in a God that turns out not to exist, then you might lose out on a life of unrestrained sensual gratification, but what is that compared with the possible bliss of eternal salvation (or, should you choose the wrong path, the eternal suffering of damnation)?

If you find such a decision difficult, or perhaps even distasteful—to reduce religious belief to a self-interested gamble—then you are not alone. However, the point is that even here the decision is up to us. Rationality or self-interest might tip the scales a little, but ultimately religious belief is not the result of a calculation. For, whatever reason decides, it is the heart—emotion, intuition, spiritual insight, whatever you may call it—that has the final say.

MEN ARE MISTAKEN IN THINKING THEMSELVES FREE.

35

BARUCH SPINOZA
1632–1677

SOURCE: *Ethics*
DATE: 1677
FIELD: Metaphysics

Descended from Portuguese Jews who had settled in Amsterdam because of its reputation for tolerance, Spinoza was even there a controversial figure, expelled from the Jewish community for his unconventional religious views. However, it is for his *Ethics* that he is most remembered, which is not—as the name misleadingly suggests—a treatise about moral philosophy, but a rational conception of the universe where everything is determined by divine necessity.

Though the exact nature of his views is contested, Spinoza is often termed a *pantheist*, believing that God and the universe were the same thing. Although God has an infinite number of aspects, we, with our limited human capacities, only experience Him via two: mind and matter. Thus, the physical universe is simply God seen from one particular perspective (as *extension* or matter), while our thoughts and feelings are God experienced from another (as mind).

While logically neat, this would seem to cause certain problems. First, everything that happens on a physical level must be mirrored on a mental level. Second, events on both levels are simply the will of God. And since God does nothing by chance, but always acts wisely and perfectly out of necessity, then everything is also fixed and preordained. There's no human free will, because all our thoughts and actions are merely expressions of divine will.

Nonetheless, Spinoza still concludes that we have freedom, because we are free to the extent that we understand the reason for our actions. It is this knowledge that sets us free, and only our ignorance that keeps us enchained.

Let us suppose
the mind to be,
as we say, white
paper, void of
all characters,
without any ideas.

36

JOHN LOCKE
1632-1704

SOURCE: *An Essay Concerning Human Understanding*
DATE: 1689
FIELD: Epistemology

What do babies know? Philosophers have long disagreed on this point, aligning themselves into two broadly opposing camps: rationalists and empiricists.

Rationalists argued that, while much knowledge comes from experience, certain important ideas do not—they are *innate* (present from birth), simply waiting for experience to draw them out. Plato, for instance, argued that, when we are born, we bring with us remnants of knowledge from our prebirth existence, where the soul had access to the true *Forms* of absolute knowledge. All education, then, is merely remembrance; we just need a prompt.

As a friend of scientist Sir Isaac Newton, English empiricist philosopher John Locke denied this. Aren't we all simply blank slates, white paper waiting for experience to write its lessons upon us? For who is born knowing "1+1=2," that God exists, or the laws of cause and effect? Even if a newborn could speak, could it tell you about Pythagoras's theorem? This, Locke argued, was patently absurd.

Yet the rationalist's point needn't depend on a belief in reincarnation or infant prodigies. It might just be, as Leibniz argued, that the mind by its very nature is fitted from birth to recognize certain fundamental truths, which run as it were *through* experience, like a vein through marble. These ideas then form a foundation for our search for more mundane knowledge. Before I can know whether it was the cat that knocked the cup off the table, I must first accept that every effect has a cause—the cup did not simply jump off by itself.

Or who is more to blame, though both of them do ill: She who sins for pay, or he who pays for sin?

37

SOR JUANA INÉS DE LA CRUZ
1651–1695

SOURCE: Poem 92, "Philosophical Satire" in *Castalian Flood*
DATE: 1689
FIELD: Feminist philosophy

Sor Juana Inés de la Cruz was a Mexican philosopher, scholar, poet, and composer who became a nun at age 18 in order to better devote herself to study. She was a prodigious child, learning to read at three before mastering Latin, and would go on to achieve fame for her literary and scientific writings, holding her own with contemporary philosophers, poets, and scientists, and even communicating with Sir Isaac Newton. She was also as fearless as she was precocious, and caused great controversy by her criticism of male hypocrisy—the subject of the poem from which the quote is taken.

If a man pays a prostitute for sex, who is more culpable? Obviously, according to contemporary standards, while both are involved in a sinful act, the primary condemnation would have fallen on the woman—just as many Christian theologians saw the Fall of Man in the Garden of Eden as due to Adam's temptation by Eve.

However, de la Cruz asks, is this fair? For is it not at least partly the fault of men in the first place, seeking an extramarital outlet for their carnal lusts, which generates a need for prostitution? It is men that create the need for "whores." And yet, having sated themselves, they then despise and blame the source of their "temptation," absolving themselves of all blame.

The 17th century was not ready for such truth-telling, especially not from a woman, and de la Cruz was censured, forced to give up her writing and endure penance for her outspokenness.

For unthinking things, to exist is to be perceived; so they couldn't possibly exist out of the minds of thinking things that perceive them.

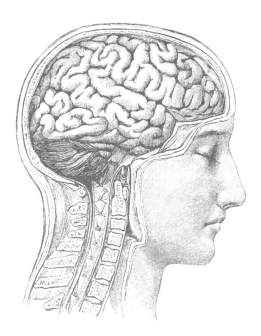

38

GEORGE BERKELEY
1685–1713

SOURCE: *A Treatise Concerning the Principles of Human Knowledge*
DATE: 1710
FIELD: Metaphysics

The mug before me has various qualities: it's red, hard, it makes a "ping" when I flick it, it's warm and smells of coffee, and so on. If I say it's also made of matter, what does this add? According to George Berkeley, Irish bishop and prominent empiricist philosopher, it adds nothing at all. All our knowledge of the mug comes either directly or indirectly through perception. We cannot perceive matter itself, only its properties. Then how do we know it exists? So, argues Berkeley, let's do away with it, and consider that all that exist are minds and their perceptions.

This position—a form of *idealism*—sounds crazy, but it makes an interesting point: If all knowledge relies on perceptions, we can't know for certain what lies *beyond or behind* them. Yet without matter, wouldn't we all just float around like spirits, passing through each other? Yet the assertion that only minds and perceptions exist doesn't imply that things aren't "solid," merely that "solidity" doesn't require the existence of matter. After all, we *perceive* that something is hard (by touch), which is therefore just another perception in the mind.

That said, few philosophers now defend Berkeley's radical position, and his argument as a whole has many flaws. If objects are simply groups of perceptions, what makes the mug a "real" object, that doesn't pop in and out of existence like something in a dream? Berkeley's answer—God—not only requires religious belief, but also raises the question of why God would so thoroughly deceive us, for doesn't it seem *natural* to assume that matter exists?

Everything possible demands that it should exist.

39

GOTTFRIED WILHELM LEIBNIZ
1646–1716

SOURCE: *The Monadology*
DATE: 1714
FIELD: Metaphysics

Gottfried Wilhelm Leibniz was a German rationalist philosopher and mathematician. Like Spinoza, who influenced him, he saw the world as a rational expression of God's will: The world is thus because it couldn't have been otherwise. This, partly, is what the quote means: Everything that's possible is also actual.

And yet, many things seem possible that *aren't* actual: My grandfather wasn't 7 feet tall; the capital of France isn't Marseille; and the Soviet Union wasn't first to land on the Moon. These things certainly seem to have been possible. So why, if Leibniz is right, didn't they happen?

However, a world in which the above things were true wouldn't be *this* world. Everything that happens, Leibniz argued, happens for a reason, and how history evolves is determined by the inherent nature of each thing in it. It might seem trivial to make someone a foot taller, or to change a country's capital, but to alter even one thing is to change everything, for everything is connected. If my grandfather were 7 feet tall, he might have chosen basketball over teaching, and might then have married someone other than my grandmother—who then might have been *someone's* grandmother, but not *mine*. So, although it is *possible* that I exist *and* my grandfather was a basketball player, those two possibilities are not compatible.

The well-known quote (which rather reflects Spinoza's position) is actually incomplete, for it continues: "[…] unless something else prevents it." For while other worlds were possible, it was only *this* world—the only one in which all possible things might exist *compatibly*—to which God granted its demand to exist.

Reason is, and ought only to be the slave of the passions.

DAVID HUME
1711–1776

SOURCE: *Treatise of Human Nature*
DATE: 1738–1740
FIELD: Ethics

Scottish empiricist philosopher David Hume greatly influenced many areas of philosophy, but one of his most original contributions was to ethics, famously stating that "'Tis not contrary to reason to prefer the destruction of the whole world to the scratching of my finger." This doesn't mean he didn't care about the world, or cared more for his finger, merely that such concern wasn't based on reason but emotion. It's through our "sentiments" that we hold things to be moral or otherwise. Theft or assault are wrong because, ultimately, we can empathize with those who might suffer such acts, and it's through our common human nature that we share the same emotional reactions.

Plato argued it was impossible for a person to knowingly do wrong, for we all aim at *what we think* is right. Wrongdoing was therefore simply a matter of ignorance. Hume, however, pointed out that reason doesn't actually determine what we should do in any situation, for moral statements are always conditional. If your friend drinks and drives, you can point out that she is endangering herself and others. If she doesn't desist, does that make her behavior irrational? No, Hume would argue, for the most reason can say is, "*If* you want to be safe, *then* don't drink and drive." Hume's insight has become known as the "is-ought gap": assault, for example, is only wrong *if* you hold the value that it is, which is supplied by emotion. Even if we agree that "Assault causes pain and suffering," we still aren't rationally compelled to admit that it is morally wrong.

Man is born free; and everywhere he is in chains.

41

JEAN-JACQUES ROUSSEAU
1712–1778

SOURCE: *The Social Contract*
DATE: 1762
FIELD: Political philosophy

Jean-Jacques Rousseau was a French-speaking philosopher and native of the Republic of Geneva (later to be the capital of Switzerland) whose ideas influenced the French Revolution of 1789, promoting the republican ideal that political authority lies primarily with the people, not with unelected rulers or hereditary kings.

The English philosopher Thomas Hobbes had thought an all-powerful monarch necessary to curb our natural human tendency to dominate each other. However, Rousseau considered human nature basically decent, and it's in this sense that we are "born free," and it's only as society develops, and political organization and authority are required, that we risk the loss of freedom. To ensure order and justice without endangering liberty, Rousseau argues for a form of democratic republic, where each person is expected to participate in deciding the laws that all the community must abide by (each joint decision constituting the "general will").

It's only through accepting personal political responsibility that people can be free. This isn't to say that such direct democratic involvement is always attainable, and even in small states some form of representative government would be necessary to ensure that the general will was enacted in day-to-day affairs—Rousseau wanted people to have their say, not to personally administer every aspect of the state. Because of such practical considerations, while not ideal, the best form of government for bigger states might be an elected aristocracy or even a monarchy. Whatever the specific form of political organization, however, its goal should always be to serve the general will. Even a king did not actually *rule*, but *serve* the people.

I DESPISE PHILOSOPHY,

**AND RENOUNCE ITS GUIDANCE;
LET MY SOUL DWELL WITH COMMON SENSE.**

THOMAS REID
1710–1796

SOURCE: *An Inquiry into the Human Mind*
DATE: 1764
FIELD: Epistemology

Does a philosopher who despises philosophy thereby cease to be a philosopher? The target of Scottish philosopher Thomas Reid's disapproval here isn't philosophy, as such, but a philosophical tradition, going all the way back to Plato, that sees a gap between human perception and reality. This has sometimes been called the "veil of perception," and it suggests that, because our perceptions are sometimes mistaken, or differ according to varying perspectives or environments, we perceive the world not directly but *indirectly,* through a sensory *representation.* This position, known as *indirect* or *representative realism,* has been defended by philosophers as diverse as Descartes and Hume, who have also recognized that it can lead to skepticism. Since we do not perceive the "real" world directly, we have no guarantee that we are not systematically deceived by our senses.

Philosophers have proposed various solutions to this problem, but Reid's answer was to abandon the distinction altogether and return to "common sense," by which he meant the set of undeniable, widely held assumptions that allow us to function and communicate in the world. Thus, we *do* in fact perceive the world directly. To take a famous example, a straight stick half-submerged in water may appear bent; yet, Reid would argue, this isn't because we don't perceive the "real" stick, but rather because *that's how straight sticks appear* under those circumstances. Objects always differ in appearance depending on certain relations—changes in viewpoint, relative size, conditions of light—but this doesn't mean there's some ideal world of straight sticks that sensory "illusions" hide from us. It's simply the way that sticks variously appear.

If God did not exist,
it would be necessary to
invent Him.

43

VOLTAIRE
1694–1778

SOURCE: "Letter to the Author of the Book, *The Three Impostors*"
DATE: 1768
FIELD: Philosophy of religion

This famous quotation has often been taken to imply that religion is a useful fiction, helpful perhaps in keeping the masses in their place. However, that is not its true meaning, which is rather that the existence of God is so fundamentally integral to the meaning of life that we cannot do without it.

Voltaire was the pen-name of François-Marie Arouet, a French philosopher, playwright, and satirist, whose attacks on both Church and state frequently landed him in trouble. However, here we find him defending religious belief, and the work in which the quote appears is itself a response to an anonymous essay of the time promoting atheism. For, as much as Voltaire was fond of pointing out the hypocrisy, superstition, and corruption of the Catholic Church, he also recognized that some form of religious belief must play a central role in both personal and public life.

For Voltaire, this belief took the form of *deism*, which accepted that some form of all-powerful force was responsible for the creation of the universe, while denying that such a force could interfere in human affairs in the miraculous way that the God of monotheism was traditionally thought to. As such, a deist did not have faith, but rational conviction, bolstered by philosophical argument. Without God, how could the universe have come into being? What would give order to the natural world? What would hold society together? Without the threat of punishment for the wicked and reward for the just, what would be the basis of morality? Could atheism fulfill that role? Voltaire thought not.

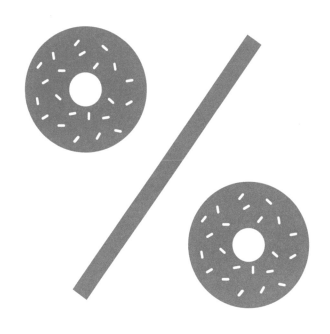

It is not from the benevolence of the butcher, the brewer, or the baker that we expect our dinner, but from their regard to their own **interest.**

44

ADAM SMITH
1723–1790

SOURCE: *An Inquiry into the Nature and Causes of the Wealth of Nations*
DATE: 1776
FIELD: Political philosophy

Economist Adam Smith, friend of Hume and fellow Scot, is often seen as a founding father of modern capitalism, providing a justification for the notion of the "free market"—that is, the idea that the economy works best when no one intervenes in its running.

There are times when it might be tempting for a government to set prices or regulate aspects of trade—to protect consumers, perhaps, by ensuring that prices aren't artificially high. Let's take the baker in Smith's example: What if he or she were to drastically increase the price of bread? Shouldn't some authority guard against that? Smith argues that no such regulation is necessary, because what keeps the baker honest—and the market in general—is his customers. If his bread is too pricey, people will shop elsewhere. It's the competition of other bakers that ensures that the price of bread is kept at a reasonable level. Therefore—as if by an "invisible hand" (to use Smith's evocative phrase)—the market regulates itself.

What about fair distribution of wealth? What's to stop successful bakers becoming rich at the expense of everyone else? Well, the thing about wealth is that people tend to want to show it off. The rich baker will buy a bigger house, perhaps, a few nice cars, some expensive art, a huge garden, and in doing so will enrich others: the real estate agent, the gallery owner and the artist, the gardener and the house decorator, and so on. The wealth therefore "trickles down" through society, and everyone benefits. At least, that's the theory.

Two things fill the mind with ever new and increasing admiration and awe, the more often and steadily we reflect upon them: the starry heavens above me and the moral law within me.

45

IMMANUEL KANT
1724–1804

SOURCE: *Critique of Practical Reason*
DATE: 1788
FIELD: Ethics

The German philosopher Immanuel Kant sought to define morality in *deontological* terms—that is, as a rational *duty*. As such, his "moral law" isn't some vague notion of "conscience," some spark of moral goodness or truth given to Adam and Eve by God before their banishment from the Garden of Eden. Rather, it's the idea that morality is determined by reason itself. Traditionally, morality deals in "should" and "should not." These things are *imperatives*, or commands: "Do not kill," "Do not steal," "Love thy neighbor," and so on.

Some moral imperatives seem less binding than others—"helping others," perhaps, or "developing yourself"—because there are many ways of meeting these duties; we can't help everyone, and shouldn't be judged for not always working on our character. In contrast, however, there are other cases where our doing or not doing certain actions may have serious moral consequences—such as theft, murder, or lying. In such cases, Kant argues, we are faced with a *categorical* imperative: We must follow the correct moral action in all circumstances, because *not* to do so leads to a rational contradiction.

For instance, if you steal from someone, because moral actions concern everyone, what you're basically saying is, "It's OK for anyone to steal." If so, however, the whole notion of property collapses—no one could own anything. The same applies to lying: If it's morally acceptable to lie, then the notions of "truth" and "falsehood" become meaningless. By *universalizing* moral precepts in this way—by asking, "What if *everyone* did that?"—then we have a rational basis for deciding what's moral.

People will not
look forward to
posterity, who never
look backward to
their ancestors.

EDMUND BURKE
1729–1797

SOURCE: *Reflections on the Revolution in France*
DATE: 1790
FIELD: Political philosophy

While those influenced by Enlightenment ideals waxed lyrical about the overthrow of the despotic and corrupt *ancien régime*, Irish philosopher and politician Edmund Burke thought that no good could come of such violent and sudden change. And, with hindsight, he may have been right. For while the French Revolution of 1789 did indeed do away with many of the evils of privilege and social inequality, what it put in their place was arguably far worse, as Maximilien de Robespierre and his fellow revolutionaries instigated a deliberate policy of "terror," which executed thousands and subjugated the general populace through fear and violence.

While he believed that a people had a right to overthrow corrupt or inept authority, as a conservative Burke favored a more gradual process of change that also respected those good things that tradition had already put in place. Unlike his Enlightenment contemporaries, Burke did not believe that the imposition of rational ideals would result in a just and fair society. However well-meaning such an attempt, it ignored the fact that much of social life was founded on the *non-rational*, or what Burke termed "prejudice." For instance, an unquestioning respect for authority or religious office seems ingrained in many societies.

Perhaps, then, it is such deep-seated values and attitudes that provide the glue that binds individuals together. There might be no apparent reason to maintain such practices—and Burke was not arguing that *all* established conventions and values should be merely accepted—but we must also accept that man is not only a rational being, but also a creature of habit.

Virtue can
only flourish
amongst
equals.

47

MARY WOLLSTONECRAFT
1759–1797

SOURCE: *A Vindication of the Rights of Men*
DATE: 1790
FIELD: Feminist philosophy

Mary Wollstonecraft was an English philosopher and writer, whose most famous work, *A Vindication of the Rights of Woman*, was a landmark in feminist philosophy. That said, it does not call for the sort of radical equality that later feminists would advocate; rather, Wollstonecraft's notion of equality is one that also seems to maintain certain traditional differences between the sexes—men and women are *not* equal in every sense—and for this reason she is often considered a forerunner of true feminism. Nonetheless, the book was important in highlighting contemporary double standards relating to gender roles, especially as regards education.

Writing shortly after the French Revolution, at a time when freedom and equality were catchphrases of those pushing for social change all over Europe, Wollstonecraft points out that such principles did not seem to extend to women. The earlier French philosopher Jean-Jacques Rousseau, whose work—as noted earlier—was central to many of the ideals of the Revolution, argued in fact that women did not really need to be as well educated as men. Better, he argued, that they should be schooled in skills that would fit them for their destined roles in life—namely, as mothers and wives—rather than fill their heads with intellectual baggage they would have no need for.

In contrast, Wollstonecraft argued that the lack of the same educational opportunities restricted women's self-development. For, while women might not equal men in all pursuits, they were surely entitled to pursue their own moral and spiritual development, in which, in the eyes of God, they were fully men's equals.

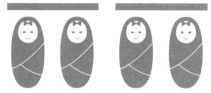

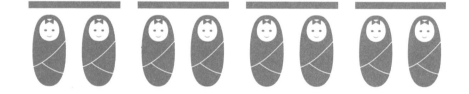

THE PERPETUAL TENDENCY IN THE RACE OF MAN TO INCREASE BEYOND THE MEANS OF SUBSISTENCE IS ONE OF THE GENERAL LAWS OF ANIMATED NATURE WHICH WE CAN HAVE NO REASON TO EXPECT WILL CHANGE.

48

THOMAS MALTHUS
1766–1834

SOURCE: *An Essay on the Principle of Population*
DATE: 1798
FIELD: Political philosophy

Let's say the average family has two children, and each of those has two children, and each of those has two children, and so on. As a result, just as computer memory is said to double every two years (Moore's law), so the rate of population growth—unless checked by outside forces—will keep on increasing exponentially.

In contrast, resources seem harder to create than babies. To get bigger crops, a farmer must plant more seeds, plow more fields, and so on. Yet each field a farmer plows doesn't then go on to create another two fields of its own! Can't science help? Better farming methods might increase crop yields, but this, combined with medical advances, will also help people live longer; so, the more food is available, the more it's likely that the population will continue to expand. Consequently, the English economist Thomas Malthus argued, a population will always outstrip its resources.

What can be done? Some things will take care of themselves. If there isn't enough food and water, people will die, or else they will fight each other for resources—so, wars for survival and other reasons will check growth. Natural disasters such as earthquakes, fires, and floods will account for others, as will diseases and epidemics. Of course, a government might try to control its population by imposing a maximum number of children (such as the "one-child policy" that used to exist in China), or by promoting contraception, abortion, or even celibacy. Yet Malthus was perhaps even more skeptical about our capacity for "moral restraint."

History is a conscious,
self-mediating process—
Spirit emptied out
into Time.

49

G. W. F. HEGEL
1770–1831

SOURCE: *The Phenomenology of Spirit*
DATE: 1807
FIELD: Metaphysics

We may tend to think of history as a fairly open-ended process, full of accidents and wrong turns, but—at least, if we're optimists—something that trends to the better. However, even an optimist is unlikely to consider history as something with a specific goal. Yet the German philosopher George Wilhelm Friedrich Hegel argued that not only does human history aim at a definite end, but its achievement of this is inevitable.

The "Spirit" referred to in the quote may be roughly thought of as some sort of universal "mind"—"God," perhaps (though there is some debate as to whether Hegel was thinking of the traditional deity). As rock pools to the sea, each individual mind or person is actually part of this overall consciousness, but simply doesn't realize it. Because of this separation from one another (*alienation*), we treat each other as rivals, forming relationships based on dominance—becoming "master" and "servant," as Hegel termed it.

However, the master–servant relationship is unstable; both are partial expressions of the whole, and, though rivals, they rely on each other. The master needs the servant to define his superiority, while the servant seeks to free himself from service. This dynamic, which Hegel uses as a metaphor for all forms of conflict and opposition, is the basic process whereby history evolves—what Hegel terms the *dialectic*. And so, conquest and revolution, growth and decline, are all steps toward the final point at which Spirit (through individuals and groups) comes to realize itself. We are all one.

EVERY NATION GETS THE GOVERNMENT IT DESERVES.

50

JOSEPH DE MAISTRE
1754–1821

SOURCE: *Diplomatic Correspondence*
DATE: 1811
FIELD: Political philosophy

Joseph de Maistre was a French-speaking philosopher from the Duchy of Savoy (an area now split between France, Switzerland, and Italy). While figures such as Locke, Hume, and Rousseau are seen as key figures in the *Enlightenment*, promoting the ideals of individual liberty, democracy, and the rule of reason over tradition, Maistre faced firmly in the other direction, arguing that a stable society could only be achieved by Christian monarchy. As such, along with such thinkers as Edmund Burke, Maistre was part of the *counter-Enlightenment*, arguing that a ruler's authority could not be based on the will of the people, who really should have no say in such matters, but was alone sanctioned by God (a long-established doctrine known as the *divine right of kings*).

Accordingly, any deviation from this ideal model was subject to divine displeasure. Maistre therefore saw the Revolution of 1789 as a punishment for the irreligious attitudes that the French aristocracy had allowed to corrupt it (namely, the philosophies of Rousseau and Voltaire). Furthermore, the resulting chaos, during which the new Republic tore itself apart in the paranoid and bloody purge (known as the Reign of Terror), was itself a divine judgment for the adoption of "atheistic" Enlightenment values (as Maistre considered them). It is in this sense, then, that every nation gets the government it deserves: A democratic republic that turned its back on royal rule thereby abandoned God, and in doing so also abandoned the divine favor that gave order and stability to society, dooming itself to anarchy and injustice.

TALENT HITS A TARGET NO ONE ELSE CAN HIT; GENIUS HITS A TARGET NO ONE ELSE CAN SEE.

51

ARTHUR SCHOPENHAUER
1788–1860

SOURCE: *The World as Will and Representation*
DATE: 1819
FIELD: Aesthetics

The German philosopher Arthur Schopenhauer was a renowned pessimist—
that is, in the strict philosophical sense. The reason for this is because, like
the Buddha, he considered desire to be the source of all our unhappiness,
and that the nature of existence was therefore characterized by suffering.
This "Will" (as Schopenhauer termed it) motivated and shaped human action,
as well as the natural world in general, forever driving all living creatures in
search of food, sex, and other desirable goals. Our only hope for happiness was
to escape the ceaseless tug of natural urges into a world of pure contemplation.
It was the ability to do this that marked out the true genius from the average
person of talent.

However, Schopenhauer thought everyone possessed some potential for
genius—if they could transcend sensual desire. As such, the best visual art did
not stimulate the baser senses, but depicted the subject in its true purity. A
landscape or a still life was often superior to a portrait or a battle scene, as the
latter often embodied some aspect of Will—the desire for beauty, the urge to
conquer or to own. Yet through the best art, the genius overcame these urges,
and—if only for a moment—glimpsed a world of pure ideas where the painful
pangs of desire almost ceased to exist. Highest art of all, however, was music,
which (unlike painting or sculpture) did not need to express itself in forms
borrowed from physical reality, and could therefore connect with and express
the deepest levels of our being—the Will itself.

PROPERTY IS THEFT!

PIERRE-JOSEPH PROUDHON
1809–1865

SOURCE: *What is Property?*
DATE: 1840
FIELD: Political philosophy

Pierre-Joseph Proudhon was a French political philosopher who is often considered the father of anarchism as a defined political philosophy. A sometime friend of communist Karl Marx (discussed later), the two would later fall out, but despite that their views have much in common. Perhaps their main point of agreement, however, concerns the nature of property under capitalism.

The goal of anarchism is not chaos—as the modern, popular use of the term might suggest—but freedom from authority. Yet, without authority, wouldn't we have lawlessness and literal anarchy? Proudhon thought not, arguing that the externally imposed, top-down authority of the state could be replaced by a loose association of individuals and small collectives, each possessing its own means of production. So, as a baker, with my own oven, I could not only bake loaves for myself, my friends and family, but trade these for other things I needed—from cattle farmers, or blacksmiths, or plumbers—based on equivalent value (the amount of time and labor involved). Furthermore, I might own land that I had cultivated or lived on.

This system, which Proudhon called *mutualism*, was therefore intended not to abolish ownership altogether, but to distinguish between *personal property* and *private property*. The products of a person's time and labor—the baker's bread, the farmer's field—are their own *personal property*, whereas a capitalist who acquires *private property*—which may be land that he never even develops—is in effect, without the sweat of his brow, "stealing" that which should be common to all.

Every law
is an evil, for
every law is an
infraction of
liberty.

53

JEREMY BENTHAM
1748–1832

SOURCE: *The Theory of Legislation*
DATE: 1840
FIELD: Political philosophy

Laws don't simply restrict freedom, however; they also grant it. Laws protect property, forbid false imprisonment or slavery, guard against physical harm, and without such protections we *wouldn't* be free. Laws also protect us from ourselves—by limiting certain activities, depending on age or capacity (drunk people and children can't drive cars). So Bentham isn't denying the necessity of such laws, merely pointing out that they are, at best, the lesser of two evils, and a restriction upon our natural ability to make ourselves happy. And it's this ability, not some abstract notion of moral goodness, that laws should ultimately serve.

Jeremy Bentham was an English philosopher and founder of *utilitarianism*, which holds that those actions are morally right that bring happiness to the greatest number. This is because what we call moral goodness *is* just happiness, and the basis of happiness is pleasure. The only justification for restricting my natural ability to maximize my pleasure is therefore to ensure maximum *overall* happiness.

I enjoy collecting art, so owning more art would make me happier. If I can't afford that, however, may I steal some from a gallery? To decide, Bentham would argue, we have to weigh up the consequences in terms of who benefits most from my theft. I obviously would, but my pleasure would have to be balanced against the "pain" of potentially getting caught, or the pleasure that visitors to the gallery would be deprived of. On balance, then, it might not be a "good" idea, and so laws forbidding this type of theft seem justifiable in utilitarian terms: Overall, they make everyone happier.

THEOLOGY IS ANTHROPOLOGY.

54

LUDWIG FEUERBACH
1804–1872

SOURCE: *The Essence of Christianity*
DATE: 1841
FIELD: Philosophy of religion

The traditional conception of God, as it appears in the monotheistic religions, ascribes to the deity qualities that infinitely surpass those of any human: God is all-knowing (*omniscient*), all-powerful (*omnipotent*), perfectly good (*omnibenevolent*), and exists everywhere (*omnipresent*). However, while these are qualities that no human could possess, they do bear a resemblance. God is a "person," who "acts," who "knows," who "wishes," and "desires" and "feels."

Consequently, the German philosopher Ludwig Feuerbach argued that the tendency to portray God in human terms (*anthropomorphism*) is actually an indication that "God" does not exist and that there is no divine reality behind these concepts, which are simply idealized and magnified projections of our own qualities. Theology, the "study" of God, is actually anthropology, the study of humanity. God is good because *we* have the potential to be so; wise because we are capable of wisdom, and so on. In worshipping these qualities in another being, we are thereby merely externalizing and alienating ourselves from what is rightfully ours. We are worshipping ourselves. Why not, then, simply recognize "God" for what "He" is, a celebration of our own ideal qualities, and reclaim them for ourselves?

Whether or not Feuerbach is right, the problem of anthropomorphism has long been recognized by theologians, who argue that we should not take such language literally, for it is simply a convenient way of depicting a divine reality that is necessarily beyond our limited human comprehension. Merely to point out, then, that religious language portrays God in human terms is not itself disproof of His existence.

It is quite true what philosophy says:
that life must be understood backward.
But then one forgets the other principle:
that it must be lived forward.

55

SØREN KIERKEGAARD
1813–1855

SOURCE: *Journals*
DATE: 1843
FIELD: Philosophy of religion

Often in life we must make decisions without a clear idea of what the outcome might be. While we may like to think of ourselves as rational beings, planning and choosing between carefully outlined courses of action, it's often the other way around: We choose out of desire, or hope, or even anxiety and fear, then think about it later.

The Danish philosopher Søren Kierkegaard is often considered one of the first *existentialists*. Before Sartre or de Beauvoir, before even Nietzsche or Heidegger, Kierkegaard was interested in the role that emotion and other "irrational" factors play in helping decide our life's choices. Deeply religious, he nonetheless rejected the idea that faith could be based on rational argument. Faced with whether or not to believe in God, not only was there no conclusive evidence that could decide for you, but our ultimate decision was always at bottom a non-rational choice—a "leap of faith" (as his attitude has often been described).

What makes Kierkegaard an existentialist is not only this emphasis on personal choice and responsibility, his contention that reason and intellectual systems cannot make our choices for us, but his analysis of the emotional and psychological states involved in this process. For instance, faced with a difficult choice, we feel "anxiety." This is not fear, as such, but a form of "existential dread," an awareness that, at bottom, we choose not from rational certainty, or external necessity, but out of our own free will. And having chosen, we try to make sense of what we have done.

Philosophers have hitherto only interpreted the world in various ways. The point is to change it.

56

KARL MARX
1818–1883

SOURCE: *The German Ideology*
DATE: 1845
FIELD: Political philosophy

From its beginnings, philosophy has actively sought a better world. Plato and Aristotle laid down principles for ideal societies, as, later on, did Bacon, Locke, and Rousseau. To imply, therefore, that philosophy had been lax in its practical duties seems rather unfair.

However, as a revolutionary socialist, German philosopher Karl Marx was making a more radical, yet more subtle point: ideas don't determine how we live; rather, how we think is determined by life—specifically, our economic relationships. The steam mill created both capitalist owners and expendable workers (the *proletariat*), and this relationship generated a legal, political, and moral framework to support and justify it. How, then, could this change? Ironically, it's the unfairness inherent in this relationship that would inevitably lead to revolution. Mistreated and exploited, the proletariat would rise up.

Unlike most previous political philosophies, Marxism is non-hierarchical, egalitarian, and materialist: An ideal communist society would have no state to tell people how to live; no bosses determining how they spent their time; no God, popes, nor priests to tell them what to think. In Marx's eyes, all social hierarchies were a means of exploitation—of the have-nots by the haves. Equality therefore required the eradication of all forms of social distinction—social classes, educated elites, politicians, and civil servants that stole power from the people they claimed to represent. Even private ownership would be abolished, all property being held in common—hence, *communism*.

After the revolution, a temporary "dictatorship of the proletariat" would dismantle capitalism and establish communism, which, historically at least, is where the theory has come unstuck.

That man is richest whose
pleasures are the cheapest.

HENRY DAVID THOREAU
1817-1862

SOURCE: *Journals*
DATE: 1856
FIELD: Political philosophy

Henry David Thoreau was an American transcendentalist philosopher famous for his writings on civil disobedience, where he considered legitimate ways in which individuals could protest against the unjust acts of the state. Transcendentalism was a philosophical and literary movement of the first half of the 19th century in America, emphasizing spirituality, individualism, and the appreciation of nature over what it saw as the excessive and sometimes dehumanizing effect of scientific rationalism. This is not to say that it was *antirational* (as perhaps may be said of its contemporary movement, *Romanticism*), but rather that it held each human to be significant—we are more than just powerless cogs in the machines of government—and stressed that meaning and dignity could be found through living a simple life close to nature in accord with the principles of self-reliance and personal moral integrity.

Thoreau himself strove hard to embody these principles, refusing to pay his taxes in protest against the government's part in the Mexican-American War and it's position on slavery. His most famous work, *Walden*, records the two-year period he spent in a cabin near Walden Pond in Concord, Massachusetts, where poetic descriptions of nature intermingle with philosophical observations on life, death, our place in the world, and much else besides. The quote, however, taken from his journals, suggests not an attempt to escape society—in his isolation, Thoreau's thoughts are as much concerned with political affairs as natural and philosophical ones—but to clarify for himself what makes life worthwhile. In truth, to be happy, we need very little.

IF ALL MANKIND, MINUS ONE, WERE OF ONE OPINION,

AND ONLY ONE PERSON WERE OF THE CONTRARY

OPINION, MANKIND WOULD BE NO MORE JUSTIFIED IN

SILENCING THAT ONE PERSON, THAN HE, IF HE HAD THE

POWER, WOULD BE JUSTIFIED IN SILENCING MANKIND.

58

JOHN STUART MILL
1806–1873

SOURCE: *On Liberty*
DATE: 1859
FIELD: Political philosophy

John Stuart Mill was an English philosopher whose political and economic views provided a cornerstone for *liberalism*. Consequently, the quote chiefly concerns defending the rights of the individual against what he terms "the tyranny of the majority." In most societies, norms and values are determined by what most people believe. As such, these beliefs will mostly determine what is legal and illegal, and what is morally or socially acceptable (or not). There is a danger then that minority views will be drowned out, or that those who hold them will be persecuted or discriminated against. After all, belief in sexual and racial equality was once a minority view, as was the notion that the Earth orbited the Sun, so simply believing with the majority is no guarantee of truth or justice. So, even if the minority is only a single person, then there is a possibility that his or her view is the right one.

What if, for the sake of argument, the minority is wrong? What if his or her view goes against the deepest-held values of society in general? Why shouldn't we silence a rabid racist, or a modern advocate of slavery? We should not, argues Mill, because even wrong views can be beneficial. Truth should not fear contradiction; in fact, this only makes it stronger. If a view is right, then its correctness is reinforced by defeating false views, and when this is done by open and rational debate, then those who hold false minority views may be converted by reason, without the need for censorship, force, or oppression.

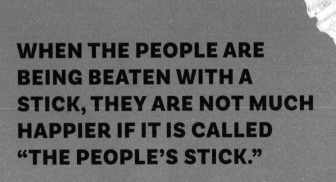

**WHEN THE PEOPLE ARE
BEING BEATEN WITH A
STICK, THEY ARE NOT MUCH
HAPPIER IF IT IS CALLED
"THE PEOPLE'S STICK."**

59

MIKHAIL BAKUNIN
1814–1876

SOURCE: *Statism and Anarchy*
DATE: 1873
FIELD: Political philosophy

While both communism and anarchism seek to wrest control of political power out of the hands of the state and into the hands of the working class, they differ as to how this should be done.

Marx denied that a just and equal society would simply spontaneously emerge from the overthrow of the powers that be; there must be a period of organized transition, a process that must be overseen by wise heads (like himself, no doubt). This seems a fair point: It's very idealistic, even naive, to assume that simply seizing control of property and industry, and dismantling the institutions of the state, would give rise to a fairer system. Something must be put in its place, and that requires planning and organization—but by whom?

The problem with Marx's solution, as Russian anarchist philosopher Mikhail Bakunin pointed out, is that it creates a new elite. Despite any protestations that their sole purpose is to usher in a new age, or that their position is only temporary, what's to stop this new authority from abusing its role? Bakunin argued—rightly, if we are to judge from Russian and Chinese history—that, given absolute power, even the most fervent revolutionary would eventually behave worse than the Tsar. Power inevitably corrupts.

Yet more importantly—the possibility of corruption aside—even if it has your best interests at heart, no such authority could *ever* be legitimate. The nature of *all* authority is to compel by force. Freedom can only result from those laws that we recognize *voluntarily.*

One must have chaos in one's soul
to give birth to a dancing star.

60

FRIEDRICH NIETZSCHE
1844–1900

SOURCE: *Thus Spoke Zarathustra*
DATE: 1885
FIELD: Ethics

The German philosopher Friedrich Nietzsche was a forerunner of *existentialism*, arguing that we must define our own values. If, as he famously proclaimed, "God is dead," then unless He is replaced with something else, humanity is left with *nihilism*: no meaning, no morality, no purpose. What should fill this God-sized hole? Nietzsche's answer was the *Übermensch* or "Superman," who would create his own values, and reinvent himself out of the old dying culture. Rather than seek these values outside ourselves, however, this new morality should spring from our own nature, our own "will to power," as he termed it, building upon the natural drives and instincts that form the basis of life itself. It was these instincts, and not the rational principles that philosophers traditionally looked to, that would provide the foundation for his new worldview.

Life is not simple or orderly, and we cannot reduce it to rational principles, much as science would like to; in fact, it was the urge to do so that was itself a sign of nihilism. In contrast to the Superman, who sought rebirth and reinvention, there was therefore also "the Last Man," who sought to reduce the spontaneous chaos of life to a neat set of equations, to make it comfortable, painless, easy, to rid it of conflict, suffering, and loss. Yet aren't these qualities essential to life? Aren't all living things in constant struggle to assert themselves, to survive, to grow and thrive? And, rather than turning our back on this chaotic process, oughtn't we rather embrace it, and so become stronger?

IT IS OFTEN SAID THAT
EXPERIMENTS SHOULD
BE MADE WITHOUT
PRECONCEIVED IDEAS.
THAT IS IMPOSSIBLE.

61

HENRI POINCARÉ
1854–1912

SOURCE: *Science and Hypothesis*
DATE: 1902
FIELD: Philosophy of science

As Henri Poincaré wasn't just a philosopher, but a mathematician, engineer, and physicist, the Frenchman's skepticism on this point shouldn't be taken as being "anti-science." Rather, he's pointing out that it's simply not possible to approach a subject without preconceptions, for, being unconscious, we may not even be aware that we have them. Why have we chosen *this* particular aspect to test? Why *this* theory, and not some other? Our very language contains within it countless assumptions that we have simply inherited in the process of learning it—words themselves can be misleading.

A related point was made by English philosopher Francis Bacon. Writing in Shakespeare's time, Bacon attempted to give science a sound philosophical basis. To do so, he argued, we must become aware of the various ways that the mind naturally distorts what it deals with. Thus, there were certain "idols" that we are prone to "worship," albeit unconsciously: We expect language to reflect reality, yet we use words carelessly ("idols of the marketplace"); we expect what we discover to fit certain inbuilt expectations we have of order and regularity ("idols of the tribe"); we may distort our findings by our own personal likes and dislikes ("idols of the cave"); or put too much trust in received wisdom ("idols of the theatre").

This doesn't mean that experiment cannot be trusted, merely that we must try to isolate such biases and misconceptions. In fact, both Bacon and Poincaré agreed, experiment is vital to science, for even our best equations are only as good as the observations that support them.

In the ethical progress
of man, mutual support—not
mutual struggle—has had
the leading part.

62

PETR KROPOTKIN
1842–1921

SOURCE: *Mutual Aid*
DATE: 1902
FIELD: Political philosophy

Despite being born into a rich aristocratic family—his father was a prince—the Russian political philosopher Petr Kropotkin was keenly aware of the great social injustice that permeated contemporary Russia, where most of its population still existed in a state of feudal serfdom.

Turning his back on his aristocratic heritage, Kropotkin embraced anarchism, emphasizing the need for social cooperation—or as he termed it, "mutual aid." Unlike Marx, who believed some form of temporary "workers' state" was necessary to transition from capitalism to communism, Kropotkin believed workers could band together in loose forms of low-level organization—cooperatives and communes—that would allow them to achieve self-sufficiency. Through this voluntary system, money would eventually be phased out, to be replaced by trade and exchange.

However, wouldn't human nature make this approach unfeasible? If, as Darwin argued, each species was engaged in a fierce struggle for survival, then without some overarching authority, wasn't it likely that certain groups would dominate over others, motivated by greed, fear, and mistrust? However, without undermining Darwin's central insight, Kropotkin persuasively argued that nature was not fundamentally driven by competition. In fact, if we look, there are many examples of cooperation—not just *within* species (the ant colony, the wolf pack), but *between* them (what biologists call *mutualism*): Bees pollinate flowers, birds eat ticks and parasites on zebras and rhinos, bacteria survive in the human gut by aiding digestion. As such examples show, nature is as much driven by "mutual aid" as by competition. If even different species can aid each other, then why can't humans?

IF I AM ASKED "WHAT IS GOOD?" MY ANSWER IS THAT GOOD IS GOOD, AND THAT IS THE END OF THE MATTER.

63

G. E. MOORE
1873–1958

SOURCE: *Principia Ethica*
DATE: 1903
FIELD: Ethics

The psychoanalyst Sigmund Freud famously proposed that humans are
instinctively driven by a "pleasure principle" to seek pleasant experiences
and avoid unpleasant ones. Nietzsche contended that all beings are motivated
by a "will to power," a biological drive for dominance and self-expression.
Utilitarians such as Jeremy Bentham have argued that a morally right action
is simply one that increases the personal happiness of the greatest number
of people.

In different ways, all such views try to define "goodness" in natural terms
(as pleasure, power, happiness). Traditionally, this is in contrast to the
assertion that moral goodness is a *non-natural* property. For instance, Plato
argued that doing the right thing was not always the same as doing what made
you feel good; in fact, there might be occasions when doing what is right might
lead to pain or suffering. Kant even argued that pleasure was irrelevant to
acting morally.

In sympathy with such views, the English moral philosopher G. E. Moore
highlighted what he called the *naturalistic fallacy*. Just because the acts we label
good are often accompanied by a certain natural property, such as pleasure, we
cannot assume that goodness simply *is* pleasure. For if this were the case, then
we could never distinguish between what is right and what is pleasurable, as we
so often do. I like ice cream, but that doesn't mean it's acceptable to steal some.
No matter how much pleasure an act brings, we can always ask, "Yet is it also
the *right* thing to do?" It's important then that "good" remains, in a sense,
undefined. Good simply is good.

YES YES YES YES YES YES
YES YES YES YES YES YES
YES YES YES YES YES YES
YES **NO** YES YES YES YES
YES YES YES YES YES YES
YES YES YES YES YES YES
YES YES YES YES YES YES
YES YES YES YES YES YES
YES YES YES YES YES YES
YES YES YES YES YES YES
YES YES YES YES YES YES
YES YES YES YES YES YES
YES YES YES YES YES YES
YES YES YES YES YES YES

**FREEDOM IS ALWAYS AND EXCLUSIVELY THE FREEDOM
FOR THE ONE WHO THINKS DIFFERENTLY.**

64

ROSA LUXEMBURG
1871–1919

SOURCE: *The Russian Revolution*
DATE: 1918
FIELD: Political philosophy

Rosa Luxemburg was a Polish philosopher and political activist, whose unflinching commitment to the socialist cause would lead to imprisonment, torture, and, ultimately, her execution. Accordingly, as a founder of modern communism, she was later considered a sort of political martyr, yet underlying her socialist ideals is a fervent belief in democracy, freedom of thought, and the right to dissent. As the quote suggests, it is these rights that underpin a truly free society.

Luxemburg had been politically engaged from a young age, and her journalistic work and activism soon landed her in trouble with the authorities. At age 17, she moved to Switzerland, then Germany, to be closer to the hub of political events, and it was in Berlin that she would eventually be jailed for antiwar activities, attempting to convince the working classes to hamper Germany's part in the war through industrial action.

During her imprisonment the Russian Revolution took place, but it was news that she treated with some ambivalence. While other socialists rejoiced, Luxemburg was quick to recognize the dangers. Within the Russian communist leadership, the Bolshevik faction (led by Lenin) was showing worrying signs of authoritarianism and intolerance, and she also feared that the popular freedoms won by the revolution would be swallowed up by the mechanism of power: Things would be essentially the same as before, merely with a different governing elite.

All of which further underlines the importance of Luxemburg's main sentiment. Even the ideals we most value should not be placed above the freedom to disagree with them.

The point of philosophy is to **start** with something so simple as not to seem worth stating, and to end with something so paradoxical that no one will believe it.

65

BERTRAND RUSSELL
1872–1970

SOURCE: *The Philosophy of Logical Atomism*
DATE: 1918–1919
FIELD: Metaphysics

Born into an aristocratic and influential British family—his grandfather, Earl John Russell, was twice British Prime Minister—young Bertrand ignored any social advantages his background might have afforded him and dedicated himself to philosophy. One of his chief contributions was to the philosophy of mathematics, where, together with fellow English philosopher A. N. Whitehead, he attempted to prove that math could be thought of as an extension of logic.

Previous mathematicians had proposed that all numbers can be thought of as *sets*. A set is simply a grouping of objects that share some common property. So, the number "one" is simply the set of all singular things (horns possessed by a unicorn, suns in our solar system); the number "two" is a set containing all couples (eyes that the average person has, wheels on a bicycle); "three" is the set of all triplets—and so on.

However, Russell saw a problem: Imagine, he said, that there is a barber whose job is to shave everyone in the town, *except* those who shave themselves. Does the barber shave himself? Well, if he shaves himself, then he cannot be shaved by the barber (himself!); but if he *doesn't* shave himself, then it's his job to! Set theory therefore results in a paradox.

Russell tried to fix the contradiction, arguably without success, but his attempt illustrates the quotation neatly: Even the simplest, most fundamental notions in philosophy and mathematics—the very foundations that we rely upon for all our knowledge—can give rise to problems that undermine everything.

Everyone is the other, and no one is himself.

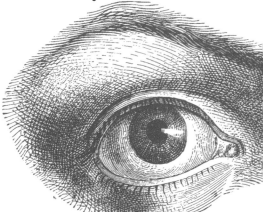

66

MARTIN HEIDEGGER
1889–1976

SOURCE: *Being and Time*
DATE: 1927
FIELD: Metaphysics

Though German philosopher Martin Heidegger's involvement with Nazism has cast a shadow over his work, his profound ideas revolutionized philosophy.

Heidegger argued that Western philosophy had lost its way, obsessing over surface level questions relating to physical reality at the expense of a deeper, more meaningful understanding of the nature of being (*ontology*). While Descartes had attempted to separate mind from body and guarantee rational certainty, Heidegger was more interested in *what it's like to be embodied*, and how our knowledge is shaped by physical activity and engagement with the world. As such, Heidegger approaches the question of being *subjectively*.

Key to this is his concept of *Da-sein*, which literally translates as "being there." Each human being is thrown into existence—a state of "being-in-the-world"— forced to make and be responsible for decisions about who and what we are, our values and beliefs. *Da-sein* therefore refers to what it's like to be *human* (that is, the type of being that's forced by the nature of its existence to make sense of itself). As such, while he refused the description, his philosophy greatly influenced existentialism.

However, while we must make existential decisions in isolation, we aren't completely alone. Each individual being also has an innate sense of "the Other." Others therefore present a necessary mirror to our self, allowing us to see who we are—but they also present a temptation. In engaging in the necessary connection with people, we also risk *losing* our authentic self—in social activities, idle chatter, trivial matters—where each becomes the "other," and no one is himself.

The traditional disputes of philosophers are, for the most part, as unwarranted as they are unfruitful.

67

A. J. AYER
1910-89

SOURCE: *Language, Truth, and Logic*
DATE: 1936
FIELD: Epistemology

In philosophy, unlike science, it's difficult to determine progress. Though Plato's theories are riddled with contradictions, fallacies, and false assumptions, philosophers still study them. Yet only historians of science are interested even in such key figures as Galileo or Newton. Why is this?

English philosopher A. J. Ayer proposed a doctrine that's become known as *logical positivism*, arguing that some philosophical questions are simply not capable of rational resolution. Ayer divided statements into two categories. Analytic statements are true because of what they mean: "All bachelors are unmarried men" is true because "bachelor" *means* "unmarried man"; "2 + 2 = 4" is true, because "2 +2" *is equivalent to* "4." In contrast, synthetic statements involve experience and experiment: We *see* the sky is blue; we *measure* a liquid's boiling point with a thermometer. If a statement doesn't fall into either of these two categories—neither true by definition nor testable—then it's either subjective or meaningless. He termed this test the *verification principle*.

If true, this consigns a great deal of philosophy—ethics, metaphysics, politics, aesthetics—to the dustbin. How could you verify the statements "All people are equal" or "Murder is wrong"? Rather, Ayer argued, ethical statements are better thought of as expressions of value: "I don't like murder," or "I don't like inequality"—which reduces ethical debate to cheering or booing.

However, there is a problem: The verification principle itself seems neither analytic nor synthetic. "Meaningful statement" and "that which can be verified" are not interchangeable terms, and it's difficult to imagine what experience might confirm the principle's truth. Does that make it subjective? Or even meaningless?

Man is nothing
else but what he
makes of himself.

68

JEAN-PAUL SARTRE
1905–1980

SOURCE: *Existentialism Is a Humanism*
DATE: 1946
FIELD: Ethics

Do we choose to be what we are? Perhaps you believe in astrology, or the idea that we are all born with certain personality types or innate dispositions; perhaps you think that, no matter what we do, there will always be some aspect of ourselves that is *not* up to us—that is, whether by nature or fate, chosen *for* us. In which case, your bad habits, your moral failings and shortcomings, are *not* all your responsibility.

If you do hold such a view, then French philosopher Jean-Paul Sartre would be in complete disagreement. In fact, as an existentialist, he would accuse you of professing *bad faith*, by which he means that you evade your moral responsibilities by believing that you are *not* free. In doing so, effectively, you give your freedom away.

However, freedom is not just the ability to do the right thing, but also to make a choice in those circumstances where there may not be a "right" answer. This is what is really meant by facing an "existential dilemma," for in such cases the correct decision is not supplied by God, by instinct, or some moral code or scheme of calculation, but is solely down to you. You are free *because* there is no "right" answer, only one that you decide is right.

Should you study law or become an acrobat? Is he the love of your life, or is someone else waiting for you? However, says Sartre, don't trust destiny or fate—they don't exist. Only choice does. Be who you choose to be.

You must not lose faith in
humanity. Humanity is an ocean;
if a few drops of the ocean are dirty,
the ocean does not become dirty.

69

MOHANDAS K. GANDHI
1869-1948

SOURCE: Letter to Rajkumari Amrit Kaur
DATE: August 29, 1947
FIELD: Ethics

Mohandas K. Gandhi was an activist and campaigner whose philosophy of nonviolent protest played a key role in bringing about Indian independence from Britain. Born into a Hindu family, he undertook legal training in London before finding work as a lawyer in South Africa. It was there that, shocked by the racial discrimination and violence that he witnessed, he began to change his political views and his stance toward British rule, developing a new political and ethical philosophy, for which he coined the term *satyagraha*.

During his time in South Africa, Gandhi had realized that the best means to bring about change was through civil disobedience and nonviolent resistance. The concept of satyagraha draws on a wide range of influences, from the writings of Henry David Thoreau and Leo Tolstoy (Gandhi corresponded with the latter) to diverse spiritual doctrines, including Quakerism, Sufism, and Jainism.

Perhaps the key idea linking these approaches is that we should lead by example: We should be the change that we wish to see. Violent activism provokes a like response, but by adopting a strategy of peaceful protest we encourage our adversaries to respond in kind. Satyagraha therefore conveys a faith in human nature. Of course, there will be times where nonviolent resistance will leave us vulnerable to the physical abuse of those still motivated by hatred and distrust. However, Gandhi argued—and as the quote beautifully illustrates—we should not let the actions and attitudes of a twisted minority prejudice us against the whole, in whom, eventually, our faith will be repaid.

It is not religion
but revolution
which is the opium
of the people.

70

SIMONE WEIL
1909–1943

SOURCE: *Gravity and Grace*
DATE: 1947
FIELD: Philosophy of religion

Karl Marx had famously portrayed religion as playing a key role in stupefying and consoling the oppressed masses, without which they would have no alternative but to acknowledge the true cause of their suffering and overthrow their capitalist oppressors. Here, French philosopher and political activist Simone Weil turns Marx's observation on its head: It's actually the desire to *escape* suffering, the illusion that we can be happy by making our lives more materially comfortable, that blinds us to the possibility of true happiness, which can only be achieved through religious salvation.

Curiously, Weil arrives at this position not as someone antagonistic to Marxism, but as a fervent socialist and trade unionist whose commitment to the plight of the working poor even led her to take on grueling factory work so as to better understand their lives. Theology has long struggled with the problem of evil—why, if God is all-knowing, all-good, and all-powerful, there is unnecessary suffering in the world. Weil's answer was that, since the world is not part of God, but something created by Him, then it is by necessity limited, mortal, and in a sense imperfect. The suffering that we all experience, to different extents, is not the consequence of divine punishment or some evil agent, but merely because we live in a world which is separate from God, ruled by impersonal physical laws and chance. However, it is such suffering that reminds us of who we really are, leading us away from the physical world toward the only source that can give our lives meaning.

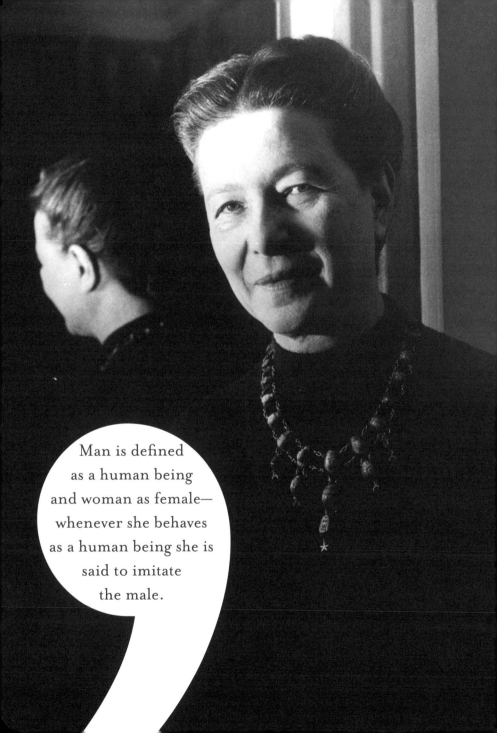

Man is defined
as a human being
and woman as female—
whenever she behaves
as a human being she is
said to imitate
the male.

71

SIMONE DE BEAUVOIR
1908–1986

SOURCE: *The Second Sex*
DATE: 1949
FIELD: Feminist philosophy

In *The Second Sex*, French existentialist philosopher Simone de Beauvoir sought to analyze why, traditionally, women had come to be seen as inferior to men. Through ancient religion and culture, and from Aristotle to Freud, the female sex had been seen as weaker, less rational, even less capable of moral responsibility, whereas men were not only seen as superior—physically, mentally, and spiritually—but even as defining what it meant to be human: "Man" stood for humanity itself.

The reason for this, de Beauvoir argued, was that women were more restricted by the body's natural functions—through menstruation and reproduction, through the associated functions and duties of child-rearing—which made it harder for them to achieve the same independence as men. Male-dominated religion and culture helped to enshrine woman's secondary status, which often saw her treated by man as a means to his own ends—as servant, cleaner, and cook, provider of sexual gratification and rearer of offspring. However, she argues, the physical differences between the sexes—which are often exaggerated—are not sufficient to relegate woman to inferiority.

As birth control and abortion liberate woman from the status of baby machines, and as equal rights and educational opportunities give them the same basis for personal growth, then it is not surprising to see women equal the achievements of men, or even surpass them. For it is not any inherent incapacity—physical or mental—that has historically relegated woman to the status of "second sex," but the self-serving attitudes of men.

If one believes in nothing, if nothing makes sense, if we can assert no value whatsoever, everything is permissible and nothing is important.

72

ALBERT CAMUS
1913–1960

SOURCE: *The Rebel*
DATE: 1951
FIELD: Ethics

Albert Camus was a French philosopher and novelist born in Algeria, then a French colony. Although often associated with existentialism, Camus actually denied that the term applied to his own philosophy, which differs from Sartre's in a number of significant ways.

However, that said, both philosophers do share some common ground, recognizing that the primary challenge for human beings is the threat of *nihilism*. If there is no God or human nature to give life any inherent meaning, then how do we face the "nothingness" at its center? Camus famously characterized the situation in which we find ourselves as *the absurd*: we seem unavoidably driven to seek meaning from a universe that is blindly indifferent to us.

What then is the answer? Like Sartre, Camus recognized that a leap into religious faith was a form of escape—an act of "bad faith," as Sartre termed it—as also was suicide, which was merely an act of surrender. However, unlike Sartre, Camus saw life more positively, and even his otherwise bleak novels celebrate simple pleasures and physical sensuality, artistic creativity, and human community. Rather, he argued, we should cultivate the attitude of the rebel. In the face of mortality and absurdity, we might yet revolt against life's meaninglessness—not by creating our own values (as Nietzsche and Sartre prescribed), but by valuing what already exists. By living life to the fullest, here and now, without denying the inescapable absurdity of our situation, or the inevitability of death, we may achieve a certain courageous acceptance—even, perhaps, happiness.

Philosophy is a battle against the bewitchment of our intelligence by means of language.

73

LUDWIG WITTGENSTEIN
1889–1951

SOURCE: *Philosophical Investigations*
DATE: 1953
FIELD: Metaphysics

Strangely for a philosopher, Wittgenstein seems to have spent much of his time trying to walk away from the subject. Born in Vienna, Austria, to a wealthy background, he came to England to study under Bertrand Russell, where his intensity and brilliance seems to have convinced his mentor that the future of philosophy lay with him.

The result of this period—the only work to be published during Wittgenstein's lifetime—was the snappily titled *Tractatus Logico-Philosophicus* (*Treatise of Philosophical Logic*), which was to prove hugely influential: First, it shifted philosophy away from metaphysical questions and toward the role played by language; second, it limited philosophy to those questions answerable by analysis. Unanswerable things included ethical, artistic, and religious questions—about which we must come to our own conclusions—but also the foundations of language and meaning. Whereas Russell had tried to reduce philosophy to math and logic, Wittgenstein argued that fundamental truths can never be communicated, only demonstrated—as he put it, "What can be shown cannot be said."

Like Kant (but in a different way), Wittgenstein argued that there were limits to our understanding, which were imposed by logic and language. It was the tendency of traditional philosophy *not* to respect this distinction—to try to "say" things about deep metaphysical questions that can only be "shown"—that he therefore considered to be at the root of most philosophical problems. Once we realize this, we see clear to a way out of the labyrinth of our confusion—and can thereafter stop doing philosophy.

No matter how many instances of white swans we may have observed, this does not justify the conclusion that all swans are white.

74

KARL POPPER
1902-1994

SOURCE: *The Logic of Scientific Discovery*
DATE: 1959
FIELD: Philosophy of science

Despite its reliance upon mathematics and complicated formulae, scientific knowledge is ultimately founded upon observation and experiment. No matter how elegant your equations, if they don't fit the data, then something's wrong. Yet even if they *do* fit, there's a problem: How do you know they'll *always* fit, or fit *everywhere*, and for *all circumstances*? This is known as the problem of induction.

If all men are mortal, and Socrates is a man, then it's certain that Socrates, too, is mortal. This is *deduction*, and, as long as your assumptions are correct (concerning human mortality and Socrates' manhood), then your conclusion is undeniable. By contrast, *induction* seeks to explain a range of instances. So, *this* swan is white, and *that* swan is white, and—well, I'm going to go out on a limb here and say that all swans are white. However, anyone familiar with swans knows they also come in black. Since induction is central to scientific knowledge, then does that mean science can't be certain? Is it even knowledge?

In contributing to this debate, the Austrian-born philosopher Karl Popper first admitted that we can never absolutely confirm a scientific hypothesis: We can't know, with certainty, what colors swans come in. However, we *can* know the opposite: that is, that not all swans are white. This may sound trivial, but it's actually very important. Science doesn't progress by confirming theories, but by *falsifying* them. Our best theories are simply those we haven't yet proven wrong, and if or when they are, we'll simply replace them with better ones.

The liberating force of technology
—the instrumentalization of things—
turns into a fetter of liberation;
the instrumentalization of man.

75

HERBERT MARCUSE
1898–1979

SOURCE: *One-Dimensional Man*
DATE: 1964
FIELD: Political philosophy

We tend to associate technology with progress. Machines make our lives easier, scientific advancement saves lives—surely, then, these are good things? While acknowledging the benefits that modern technological society had brought about, German-born philosopher Herbert Marcuse nonetheless noted that it also perpetrated subtler and more profound forms of harm: While seeming to liberate us, technology actually enslaved us.

In modern capitalist society, together with the right to vote and freedom of speech, it's tempting to think of the ability to buy goods and services as an expression of individual liberty: The fact that we can buy, say, and do what we want (within legal limits) is what makes us free. Yet, Marcuse asked, do we really need the things that we are "free" to buy? How many of these purchases represent genuine needs and wants? Arguably, few. We think that our wanting a better car, a bigger house, or a new phone are free expressions of our own desire, whereas in fact these "needs" are subtly implanted by advertising and the media. In turn, in order to afford these things, the average person must work longer and harder. And so, ultimately, our desires for these apparently free purchases are merely the means whereby those who govern society may control and exploit us, keeping us quiet with consumerist dreams while getting rich off the profit of our labor.

All of this was foreshadowed by Marx himself. Marcuse's contribution was to show how, even in a flourishing, luxury-rich society that *seems* to embody democratic and liberal ideals, this freedom is merely an illusion.

Possibly the queerest of all the queer things in this life is that we should find this life so very

Queer

76

J. N. FINDLAY
1903–1987

SOURCE: *The Discipline of the Cave*
DATE: 1966
FIELD: Philosophy of religion

John Niemeyer Findlay was a South African philosopher who developed a form of what has been called "rational mysticism." In this he was influenced in part by *phenomenology*, an approach pioneered by German philosopher Edmund Husserl, and later developed by Heidegger, which attempts to deal with philosophical questions *subjectively*, in terms of *how* we experience the world—the *phenomena* of our experience. Husserl's insight was that our perceptions of the world are not neutral, but involve a certain *intentionality*. We don't just "see" a cup or a book, we see it in terms of *what it means to us*, *how we feel about it*, or *how we intend to use it*. This intentionality therefore, in a sense, *colors* all our perceptions.

In describing his approach as "rational mysticism," Findlay wished to use phenomenology to provide a possible understanding of religious and mystical states. In fact, he argued, to different degrees, we are *all* capable of such states, which arise naturally as aspects of our everyday conscious experience, and may even suggest the possibility of a sort of higher insight into the traditional puzzles of philosophy. Who has not, at times, been struck mid-sentence by the sheer "oddness" of a familiar word, paused in wonder at some common sight, or felt the sudden absurdity of some long-performed routine? This sense of the "queer" is therefore the basis of philosophy. Yet, although they may be more prone to such perceptions, it's not only poets, philosophers, and mystics who may feel life's queerness, but any and everyone. The real mystery, then, perhaps, is why in fact we do.

THERE IS NO OUTSIDE-TEXT.

77

JACQUES DERRIDA
1930–2004

SOURCE: *Of Grammatology*
DATE: 1967
FIELD: Cultural theory

The French philosopher Jacques Derrida was the prime exponent of an approach known as *deconstruction*. Like Barthes and Foucault, he had moved away from an early interest in structuralism, and his views are considered a form of *post-modernism*.

Post-modernism is itself difficult to define, which is perhaps fitting, because the one thing that may be safely said about it is that it is an approach that is skeptical of definitions! Accordingly, Derrida held that no approach to a subject can be absolutely objective, independent, or free of prejudice, because any approach will bring with it its own hidden values and assumptions.

Much of Derrida's work is concerned with "deconstructing" the central works of Western philosophy, taking apart their arguments to reveal their inherent contradictions, omissions, and biases. In doing this, however, he claims that he is not advocating his own perspective—which would, by the logic of his own position, merely entail a fresh set of assumptions and biases—but in fact using the text against itself. For, as the quote says, there can be no "outside-text" (no privileged position from which to assess another viewpoint).

In his use of the word "text" here, some of Derrida's critics have identified what they take to be the contention that language is the only reality (a position known as *linguistic idealism*). Derrida denied this, but it's an interesting criticism: Because all descriptions of reality require language, which shapes (and perhaps *mis*-shapes) the world, then there is in fact no independent reality to which we can appeal to settle matters. We are stuck inside our own "texts," and cannot get out.

In societies
where modern
conditions of
production
prevail, all of life
presents itself
as an immense
accumulation
of spectacles.

78

GUY DEBORD
1931-1994

SOURCE: *The Society of the Spectacle*
DATE: 1967
FIELD: Cultural theory

Guy Debord was a French philosopher and founding member of Situationist International, an intellectual, artistic, and political movement that presented a radical criticism of contemporary society.

Debord's classic work, *The Society of the Spectacle*, was a key influence upon 1960s counterculture, especially among students, whose protests in May 1968 ignited such civil unrest that France's leaders feared a fresh revolution. Its opening lines, from which the quote is taken, deliberately echo Marx's *Capital*, but whereas Marx saw society as dominated by the products of capitalism—"an immense accumulation of commodities"—Debord proposed that modern society had become dominated by images.

Marx argued that, in order to create profit, capitalism must sustain itself by making us discontented with our lives. As such, we become *alienated* from the products of our labor; work no longer merely supports our existence, but earns wages to buy the products of the capitalist economy—its "commodities." Debord agrees, but asserts that modern society takes this further: In the media, such commodities are replaced by representations or images whose desirability is more intangible. To illustrate Debord's point: Advertising now portrays thinness as attractive, but thinness isn't necessarily desirable in itself—in other ages, where it suggested poverty, fuller figures were preferred, indicating wealth. Yet, in the language of images that permeates modern society—"the spectacle" that determines how people see and relate to one another—being thin is desirable by association (the sense of privilege and class distinction that it conveys). In modern media-saturated society, we are even more alienated than Marx supposed: Our true connection with life is replaced by illusion.

The real question is not whether machines think but whether men do.

79

B. F. SKINNER
1904–1990

SOURCE: *Contingencies of Reinforcement: A Theoretical Analysis*
DATE: 1969
FIELD: Philosophy of mind

Sigmund Freud, the father of psychoanalysis, wanted to be taken seriously as a science, but his approach to the study of the mind was ultimately subjective. Patients reported their thoughts, feelings, dreams, and opinions, and the therapist interpreted them. Both sides of this process were therefore open to bias, distortion, and vagueness.

Therefore, American psychologist B. F. Skinner proposed, since we can't know what goes on *inside* the mind (at least, not scientifically), we should treat it as a mysterious entity, a "black box," and concentrate instead on a subject's external *behavior*. Thus *behaviorism*, as it became known, focused solely on those factors that *conditioned* behavior. As a child, you are frightened by a large owl, and thereafter you develop a phobia of birds. To remove this, we needn't interpret your dreams or analyze your relationships with your parents, but merely *recondition* you, removing the original conditioning and replacing it with a more positive attitude to birds.

The success of this approach led Skinner to think of humans as biological machines that could be easily reprogrammed. People had, as such, no free will, and their behavior, attitudes, and opinions could all be traced to either instinct or past conditioning. Was he right? In its strongest sense, behaviorism even denies consciousness, assuming that any "internal" experiences are illusory, and that mental beliefs play no part in decisions and actions. Aside from denying what seems obvious (that we are conscious), if the mind *is* a "black box," we *can't prove* that mental states play no role, and so—rather unscientifically—behaviorism rests on an unprovable assumption.

Freedom for the wolves has often meant death to the sheep.

80

ISAIAH BERLIN
1909–1997

SOURCE: *Four Essays on Liberty*
DATE: 1969
FIELD: Political philosophy

Russian-born philosopher Isaiah Berlin famously outlined two concepts of liberty—that is, political freedom: the negative and the positive. We benefit from negative freedom when no one interferes with what we think and do. Liberal Western democracies such as the USA have been traditionally held up as exemplars of this approach, ensuring individual liberty against the power of the state, because they have enshrined in their constitutions and laws the freedom of thought and lawful behavior.

Yet is this all there is to freedom? If, in bringing up a child, I do not clothe or feed it, but leave it to fend for itself, then it will be little defense to say that I am leaving untouched its "negative freedom." Berlin therefore pointed out that freedom must also have a positive aspect: To be full members of society, to grow and flourish and make the most of our innate talents and opportunities, society must help us to some degree.

Of course, all this is a matter of emphasis and balance. Positive freedom can go too far, it may be argued, when—out of concern for its citizens' well-being and growth (their positive freedom)—a state resorts to surveillance, compulsion, censorship, and indoctrination (such as in the old Soviet Union, from which Berlin was himself an émigré). Similarly—and it's this excess that Berlin is attacking in the quote—in promoting unregulated free-market capitalism, thus allowing the greedy and immoral, the already powerful (the "wolves"), to dominate the weak or less fortunate (the "sheep"), we may take negative freedom too far.

```
        $ $
       $ $ $ $
      $ $ $ $ $ $
     $ $ $ $ $ $ $ $
    $ $ $ $ $ $ $ $ $ $
   $ $ $ $ $ $ $ $ $ $ $ $
  $ $ $ $ $ $ $ $ $ $ $ $ $ $
 $ $ $ $ $ $ $ $ $ $ $ $ $ $ $ $
$ $ $ $ $ $ $ $ $ $ $ $ $ $ $ $ $ $
$ $ $ $ $ $ $ $ $ $ $ $ $ $ $ $ $ $ $ $
$ $ $ $ $ $ $ $ $ $ $ $ $ $ $ $ $ $ $ $ $ $
$ $ $ $ $ $ $ $ $ $ $ $ $ $ $ $ $ $ $ $ $ $ $ $
```

IT MAY BE EXPEDIENT BUT IT IS NOT
JUST THAT SOME SHOULD HAVE LESS
IN ORDER THAT OTHERS MAY PROSPER.

81

JOHN RAWLS
1921–2002

SOURCE: *A Theory of Justice*
DATE: 1971
FIELD: Political philosophy

The American Dream is built upon the twin ideals of freedom and meritocracy. In a free society, anyone may pursue their ambitions, and each gets what he deserves. However, this creates inequality: The successful flourish while the unsuccessful struggle. However, if that outcome is based on merit, and everyone has the same opportunity to succeed, then—inequality aside—can we really say it's unfair?

As American political philosopher John Rawls argues, we *don't* all start from the same place. By birth or luck, some possess certain advantages—education, wealth, talent, a steady and supportive home life—whereas others lack these, or even have to deal with problems that hamper them—poverty, abusive parents, trauma, tragedy. Therefore, to redress this inequality of opportunity, we should put in place certain "principles of justice" (as Rawls called them) that ensure that everyone has an equal chance. This might imply, for example, taxing the rich in order to support public health or education programs, or ensuring that all occupations are open to everyone, regardless of creed, race, or gender.

Yet don't these principles simply punish the privileged and the talented? Why should I be denied the opportunity to benefit from my lucky start? Well, says Rawls, imagine that you didn't know what race, sex, or social status you were to have in life, and, from behind a "veil of ignorance" (as he terms it) you had to choose how the society you were to be born into should be governed. Wouldn't you choose principles that would ensure you the best opportunities, no matter *who* you were?

From each as they choose,

to each as they are chosen.

82

ROBERT NOZICK
1938–2002

SOURCE: *Anarchy, State, and Utopia*
DATE: 1974
FIELD: Political philosophy

Robert Nozick was an American political philosopher whose *Anarchy, State, and Utopia* was a direct response to John Rawls' *A Theory of Justice*. Whereas Rawls' "distributive justice" only justified the advantages of the best-off if these also benefited the worst-off, Nozick responded that you cannot redistribute wealth without also compromising freedom. Accordingly, it is unfair to tax the rich to benefit the poor, and government should be solely limited to ensuring those basic necessities that enable society to function—to ensure that contracts are honored, crimes prevented, individual rights protected, and the country itself defended from outside aggressors.

Doesn't this justify inequality? Nozick argued that inequality was a natural expression of the different degrees to which we benefit from our own hard work, and we need only ensure that we get what we're entitled to. His "entitlement theory," as it's been called, therefore focuses only on how individuals acquire wealth, property, advantage, and in what ways they may do so justly.

Nozick was a *libertarian*, and his work has become the cornerstone of right-wing political groups and those who argue for minimal government and free-market economics. In truth, Nozick's position was actually closer to anarchism than conservatism—not true anarchism, perhaps, because he believes that some state governance is necessary, yet one which favors the liberty of the individual. In fact, this is the significance of the quote—deliberately echoing the Marxist slogan, "From each according to his abilities, to each according to his needs," which emphasizes not externally imposed equality, but individual freedom of choice.

I want to know what it is
like for a bat to be a bat.

83

THOMAS NAGEL

b. 1937

SOURCE: "What Is it Like to Be a Bat?" in *The Philosophical Review*
DATE: 1974
FIELD: Philosophy of mind

The "mind–body problem" concerns how the mental relates to the physical. Descartes's approach—*dualism*—considered mind and body as completely separate substances, one material, one immaterial. So, how do they interact? Modern philosophers therefore prefer *physicalism*: "Mind" is simply a certain arrangement of neurons in the brain that in some way creates or embodies mental states.

There are different varieties of physicalism, but all face a similar problem: If the mind is basically an arrangement of physical parts, then how does it become conscious? American philosopher Thomas Nagel argued that current forms of physicalism fail because they cannot account for aspects of subjective experience—what are termed *qualia*. He illustrates his argument by asking what it's like to be a bat. Our first response is to imagine what it might be like for *me* to be a bat, just as I might imagine being a Hollywood actor.

However, unlike Hollywood actors (perhaps!), bats have a fundamentally different way of perceiving the world—through echolocation. They sense the world in terms of sound, building up an aural landscape via clicks and echoes. As such, it seems fair to admit that we *don't* know what it's like to be a bat, for we can't know what it's like *for a bat* to be a bat! Their inner, subjective reality remains hidden from us. As for bats, so for humans. Thus, there's always "something it is like" to be conscious that a purely objective analysis (for example, a brain scan) can't capture. This doesn't mean physicalism is wrong, merely that current versions of it seem incomplete.

THE BELIEF
THAT HUMAN
LIFE, AND ONLY
HUMAN LIFE,
IS SACROSANCT
IS A FORM OF
SPECIESISM.

84

PETER SINGER
b. 1946

SOURCE: *Animal Liberation*
DATE: 1975
FIELD: Ethics

Most cultures accord humans a different status to animals. Often, this has a religious basis: Humans possess a soul, whereas animals do not. Furthermore, the philosopher Descartes argued that humans possess reason, which allows them to think and communicate, while animals have only basic behavioral capacities, which at best merely resemble human rationality.

In contrast, Darwin argued that humans are merely highly evolved animals, and the difference is simply one of degree. Australian moral philosopher Peter Singer agrees, claiming that to treat animals differently is a form of "speciesism," and therefore no less objectionable than racism or sexism. In fact, it seems bizarre to relegate gorillas, dolphins, and elephants to the same class of being as mollusks and shrimps, when their similarities with humans are much greater than their differences. Furthermore, their communication and reasoning skills are in fact much more advanced than philosophers such as Descartes thought. And besides, as Jeremy Bentham put it, the issue is not whether animals can think, but whether they can *feel*.

Singer shares Bentham's utilitarian perspective. To include them in a moral calculation, he argues, we needn't think of them as "persons" (a condition Kant insisted on)—though perhaps some may pass that test—but merely acknowledge that they feel pain and pleasure, happiness and sadness. However, since utilitarianism argues that the right moral choice is one that brings the greatest happiness to the greatest number, then not only may that occasionally justify animal suffering (experimentation for Alzheimer's research, for instance), but human suffering too.

A claim for equality of material position can be met only by a government with totalitarian powers.

85

FRIEDRICH HAYEK
1899–1992

SOURCE: *Law, Legislation, and Liberty,* vol. 2
DATE: 1976
FIELD: Political philosophy

In many respects, equality seems like an obviously desirable quality. Modern democracies embody the notion that everyone has the same rights, the same protections under the law, and—certain exceptions aside—one person shouldn't be treated differently to another. It may seem strange then to argue that there are circumstances where equality is undesirable.

Born in Austria-Hungary, economist F. A. Hayek fled fascism to become a British citizen just before World War II. While they differed in other respects, Hayek recognized that both Hitler and Stalin believed state control of the economy was necessary to ensure prosperity—a policy which, Hayek argued, could only lead to disaster.

Like Adam Smith, Hayek advocated a free market: Left alone, the market would regulate itself through the mechanism of supply and demand. Rather than fixing prices, we should observe how they rise or fall—the "price signal"—which gives us real-time information regarding a commodity's desirability. A drop in the price of coal may signal a glut in the market, and production should be scaled back. Yet central planning robs us of this information, restricting the market's ability to respond naturally and quickly.

However, authoritarian economic control also limits social freedom. In fixing prices and production, trying to ensure equality of material possessions, the state must also interfere in cultural and personal affairs, because the social and economic are closely intertwined. And so, while authoritarian control relegated individuals to cogs in a giant machine, stifling innovation and stunting technological progress, free-market capitalism freed both individual and society to progress and thrive.

And the woman?
She "doesn't exist."
She adopts the disguise
that she is told to put on.
She acts out the role
that is imposed
on her.

86

LUCE IRIGARAY
b. 1930

SOURCE: *This Sex Which Is Not One*
DATE: 1977
FIELD: Feminist philosophy

Born in Belgium, French feminist philosopher Luce Irigaray draws upon psychoanalysis, linguistics, and Marxism to argue that the concept of femininity has been created and applied through history to satisfy men. As the quote suggests, sexual difference does not really exist (in nonbiological terms), and the idea that "men are from Mars, women are from Venus" (to borrow the title of a popular book) has arisen only because men have defined themselves as free, conscious, thinking subjects, thereby relegating women to those qualities from which they wish to escape—the "other." As such, while men have considered themselves the prime creative force, responsible for culture and art, women have traditionally been associated with nature and physical existence, being allotted the primary role of motherhood.

The consequence of this, Irigaray argues, is that even academic disciplines such as psychoanalysis and philosophy have been skewed by the male perspective, not only physically minimizing the presence and prominence of women in its ranks, but also enshrining a male viewpoint within the very language and concepts used. Even general culture (shaped by the "male" perspective) limits the ability of women to genuinely express themselves, and modern capitalist society treats woman merely as a commodity.

What is the answer? Both "maleness" and "femaleness" have been shaped by society and culture, and it is therefore not just women who are trapped. Rather, society itself needs to create conditions for both sexes to free themselves from the false identities and opposing roles that currently define and constrict them.

THE TEXT IS PLURAL
THE TEXT IS PLURAL
THE TEXT IS PLURAL
THE TEXT IS PLURAL
THE TEXT IS PLURAL
THE TEXT IS PLURAL
THE TEXT IS PLURAL
THE TEXT IS PLURAL
THE TEXT IS PLURAL
THE TEXT IS PLURAL
THE TEXT IS PLURAL.

87

ROLAND BARTHES
1915–1980

SOURCE: *Image—Music—Text*
DATE: 1977
FIELD: Cultural theory

Structuralism was a philosophical doctrine that came to prominence in France in the second half of the 20th century and was applied to fields as diverse as sociology, anthropology, and literary theory. If you want to understand something, a structuralist would argue—whether that's a modern novel or the myth of some African tribe—look at its structure. Many fairy-tales have heroes or heroines, wicked stepparents and magical helpers. We can therefore best understand them through identifying these common elements, these structural units, and analyzing the roles they play.

In *Mythologies*, French philosopher and literary theorist Roland Barthes applied structuralism to popular culture, to such things as magazine advertising, professional wrestling, and the French love of wine. What do these things mean? Barthes argued that they were modern myths, and that we should therefore consider them structurally, as an anthropologist might, in terms of the social functions they performed.

However, Barthes' later work moves beyond structuralism, and so along with such thinkers as Derrida and Foucault (covered later) he is generally considered a *post-structuralist*. While structural analysis is a useful tool, we should not look to it to provide a definite, fixed meaning, because no such meaning exists. A novel, for instance, has innumerable influences and forces that work upon its composition, over which the author has no definitive control—he is "dead" (as Barthes famously put it). As such, not just because it can be interpreted in many ways, but also because it is made up of many things, the text is "plural."

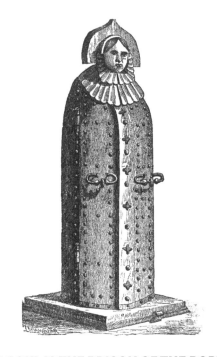

THE SOUL IS THE PRISON OF THE BODY.

88

MICHEL FOUCAULT
1926–1984

SOURCE: *Discipline and Punish*
DATE: 1977
FIELD: Cultural theory

Religions have mostly held the opposite view: It is the physical body that is traditionally the prison of the immaterial soul, suffering and enslaved by its desires, pains, and pleasures. By turning this view on its head, the French post-structuralist philosopher Michel Foucault proposed that it is actually the "soul" that "imprisons," via the concepts and categories that society uses to understand and control natural bodily functions and desires.

In moving away from his early involvement with structuralism (considered previously), Foucault came to apply his central insight to such subjects as madness, sexuality, and crime. His central contention was that theory and practice are not separate: A government does not just exercise power in the way it treats criminals or the insane, but also via the very categories that allow it to consider them as such.

Within society, individuals are granted rights under the law. Yet the law also determines the rules of property, distinguishes between private and public, and permissible and illegitimate behavior, and in doing so defines and limits what an individual *is*. In this sense, schools as much as prisons, hospitals as much as mental asylums, are all shaped by the need for political authority to keep the individual subject to society's whims. By the time you are born, there is a sense in which who "you" are has already been determined by political and legal structures that were already in place, and over which it will be extremely difficult for your growing self to have any say—for "you" will already have been shaped by society.

The sad truth is that most evil is done by people who never make up their minds to be good or evil.

89

HANNAH ARENDT
1906–1975

SOURCE: *The Life of the Mind*
DATE: 1978
FIELD: Ethics

As a German-born Jewish intellectual, Hannah Arendt had been forced to flee Nazi Germany before the Second World War, and the shadow of this experience shaped her intellectual life. Her subsequent writings investigated various political topics—totalitarianism, political freedom, power, and violence—but it is for her coverage of the 1961 trial of Nazi war criminal Adolf Eichmann that she is most widely remembered.

Eichmann had been centrally responsible for the logistics of the Holocaust, overseeing the rounding up and transportation of Jews and other "undesirables" to the death camps. His defense for this was that he was simply following orders, yet—as Arendt observed—he seemed to display no guilt or genuine remorse, his defense being that he could not be blamed for what was then his lawful duty (Hitler's policies). It was such ignorance of the despicable nature of his heinous crimes, together with his apparent lack of zealotry or psychosis (unlike other war criminals involved in the atrocities), that led Arendt to coin the now well-known phrase "the banality of evil." In other words, we expect evil people to be monstrous in some way, but what if their monstrosity merely lies in their possession of normal flaws—cowardice, prejudice, lack of empathy—and it is only the circumstances that make these qualities monstrous?

The quote is from a posthumous work, where, late in life, Arendt is still struggling to come to terms with humanity's potential for evil, and what role conscience and morality can play in helping us to avoid it.

Animals are not machines; one of my main concerns is to combat this notion.

Actually only machines are machines.

90

MARY MIDGLEY
b. 1919

SOURCE: *Beast and Man: The Roots of Human Nature*
DATE: 1979
FIELD: Philosophy of mind

In *Beast and Man*, English philosopher Mary Midgley argued that human beings share greater kinship with animals than philosophers have generally admitted, a gap that is much narrower than traditionally supposed. Animals aren't, as Descartes thought, merely unfeeling automata, and it's therefore fruitful to use our understanding of their behavior to throw light on human nature.

Yet Midgley also wished to resist a growing trend in *sociobiology* (the use of evolutionary theory to explain society and human behavior), which proposed— as if Descartes's failing was lack of courage—that *both* human and animal behavior was *mechanistic*: Not just animals are machines, but humans too. As evolutionary biologist Richard Dawkins supposes, human behavior may be reduced to the influence of our "selfish genes," which seek only to perpetuate themselves through driving us to reproduction, thereby ensuring their survival.

However, Midgley argued, neither human nor animal behavior can be reduced in this way, for motivation in either case is a very complex matter and not something we can simply reduce to the dictates of our DNA. Do your genes tell you which way to vote in an election, or which books you enjoy reading? This isn't to say that there aren't reasons for both these sorts of behavior, or even that they can't be predicted, but simply to state that understanding them is better done through traditional biological and psychological concepts. We act as we do because we *want* or *desire* something, find it *enjoyable* or *meaningful*. Our genes might ultimately program us to seek those general things, but they do not provide the final say.

#TruthIsWhatYourContemporariesLetYouGetAwayWith.

91

RICHARD RORTY
1931–2007

SOURCE: *Philosophy and the Mirror of Nature*
DATE: 1979
FIELD: Epistemology

Philosophy has traditionally held that truth is an objective matter. Plato compared it to the Sun, a source of knowledge distinct from individual conceptions and perceptions that all philosophers might independently discover. Not all, however, have agreed with him. In fact, it's this picture of an independent reality "mirrored" by philosophy that American pragmatist philosopher Richard Rorty explicitly attacked.

As a philosophical movement, pragmatism originated in 19th-century USA with such philosophers as William James and John Dewey. Rejecting both skepticism and the search for absolute certainty, pragmatists argued that beliefs should be judged on their practical benefit—that is, how successful they prove in helping us to live our lives. Perhaps we can't prove that we don't live in an illusory dream world, that we have free will, or decide whether God exists, but, taking our cue from scientific method, we may evolve concepts and explanations that serve as tools to further practical knowledge.

In his *Philosophy and the Mirror of Nature*, from which the quote is taken, Rorty combines the pragmatist approach with the ideas of Ludwig Wittgenstein (considered earlier) to argue that many of the traditional problems of philosophy are in fact not problems at all, but a result of taking philosophical ideas too seriously. Philosophy does not, as Plato argued, establish absolute truth; instead, philosophical ideas are more like metaphors that help us to understand reality. Which metaphors are best? Those that work; and, in judging their usefulness, it is the cultural community of which we are a part that decides which ideas are "true."

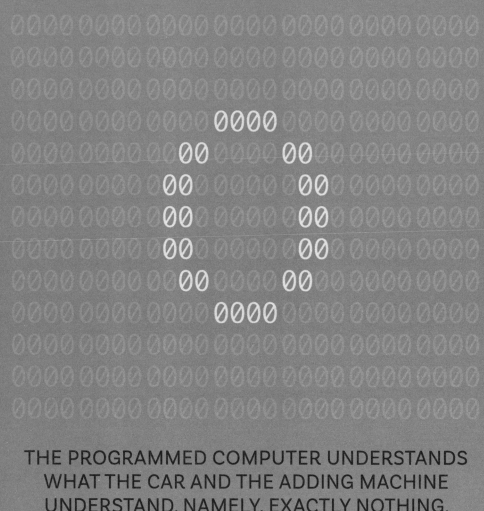

THE PROGRAMMED COMPUTER UNDERSTANDS
WHAT THE CAR AND THE ADDING MACHINE
UNDERSTAND, NAMELY, EXACTLY NOTHING.

92

JOHN SEARLE

b. 1932

SOURCE: "Minds, Brains, and Programs" in *Behavioral and Brain Sciences*
DATE: 1980
FIELD: Philosophy of mind

Famously, the English mathematician Alan Turing proposed a test: If a machine could fool us that it was human, then there would be no reason not to consider it to be "thinking." Certain believers in the potential of artificial intelligence go further than this, arguing that the increasing complexity of computers will one day mean that not only can machines think but can be considered "persons."

And yet, American philosopher John Searle argues, a computer is only a machine. Your calculator, your toaster, or your car don't "think" or "understand," in any normal sense of those words, so why shouldn't we also think that about even very complex computers? Computers follow rules, but understanding is about more than rule-following. In a famous thought experiment, Searle asks us to picture a man in a room with two hatchways. Through one hatchway come cards with Chinese characters on. The man looks up these symbols in a book, which tells him which Chinese characters to send out through the other hatch. In doing so, does he understand Chinese? Most people would say not. He is merely following rules that allow him to give responses that make sense in Chinese, but that doesn't give him any understanding of the language.

Searle's point is that this is what a computer does. So, even if a computer could pass Turing's test, this would not mean that it had understanding, or consciousness, or was a person. We might grant that it "thinks," in a limited sense of that word, but then so would the calculator, the toaster, and the car.

I AM NOT SURE THAT I EXIST, ACTUALLY. I AM ALL THE WRITERS THAT I HAVE READ, ALL THE PEOPLE THAT I HAVE MET, ALL THE WOMEN THAT I HAVE LOVED; ALL THE CITIES I HAVE VISITED.

I?

93

JORGE LUIS BORGES
1899–1986

SOURCE: Interview in *El País* newspaper
DATE: September 26, 1981
FIELD: Philosophy of mind

What is the self? Is it, as Descartes argued, the rational soul, a conscious thinking essence that defines who we truly are? Or, as Buddhism would seem to suggest, and Hume later agreed, an illusion, a mere collection of impressions and perceptions with no real center?

Here, Argentine writer and poet Jorge Luis Borges seems closer to the latter view—naturally, perhaps, for a writer of fiction, who becomes accustomed to creating and imaginatively inhabiting different characters. Borges' work, which consists mostly of short stories, is deeply philosophical, and it frequently plays with literary conventions, blurring fact and fiction, memoir and fantasy, the genuine and the fake, in order to undermine the idea of a fixed, objective reality that—even if such a thing exists—it may be beyond our ability to know.

In "The Book of Sand," a mysterious illustrated book written in an unknown language appears never to reveal the same page twice. In "The Library of Babel," the narrator lives in an infinite library, where every book presents a slightly different arrangement of the letters of the alphabet, and therefore (theoretically) every possible book that has and ever could be written, and so must contain somewhere the answers to the ultimate questions. Overwhelmed with the possibility of finding truth, the library's patrons retreat into superstition and despair.

Borges' vision, while often surreal and magical, is also therefore deeply skeptical. In questioning the nature of the self, he is implying that this, too, is a form of fiction—simply another story that we tell ourselves.

We ought not to do to
our future selves what
it would be wrong to do
to other people.

94

DEREK PARFIT
1942–2017

SOURCE: *Reasons and Persons*
DATE: 1984
FIELD: Ethics

While different in other respects, the two main forms of moral philosophy—
Kant's deontological approach and Bentham's utilitarianism—both consider
right and wrong in relation to others. These "others" might be hypothetical
people—when we ask whether it's wrong to steal from someone, we may not
have anyone specific in mind—but it's generally assumed that, whoever they
are, the other person is living right now. This is because, strictly speaking, we
cannot harm either those who are dead, nor those who are yet to be conceived.

Immoral acts often involve harm. For instance, Kant argues that stealing from
someone harms their right to pursue their own legitimate goals (if you steal
my money, I may not be able to buy food). Similarly, a utilitarian might argue
that theft deprives someone of the means to increase their happiness and
pleasure. From both points of view, however, the people whose rights or
interests are damaged must exist.

However, if they continue, current trends in climate change and
overpopulation may drastically affect the quality of life of future people,
even perhaps endangering their future existence. Neither Kant nor
utilitarianism seems equipped to deal with this; in fact, English philosopher
Derek Parfit argues utilitarianism even justifies doing nothing—what he
terms "the repugnant conclusion": Whatever the average quality of life for
the current population, we can always imagine a larger population with a
worse average quality of existence, whose total happiness is equal or higher
because of its larger size. Since, for utilitarianism, more happiness is always
better, there's seemingly no incentive not to keep adding more people.

ARE THERE OTHER WORLDS THAT
ARE OTHER WAYS? I SAY THERE ARE.

DAVID K. LEWIS
1941–2001

SOURCE: *On the Plurality of Worlds*
DATE: 1986
FIELD: Metaphysics

"World" may be used in various senses: a planet (Mars), everything that exists (the universe), some aspect of experience (the mental world), and so on. So when American philosopher David Lewis claims that other "possible worlds" exist, it's important to know that by "worlds" he means something resembling our current physical universe—only different. We should also be clear that these aren't worlds that *might* have existed, but for some reason don't. Leibniz talked of this being "the best of all possible worlds," chosen by God over other possible ones. Yet in Leibniz's sense, these possible worlds never existed outside God's mind.

A similar idea arose in quantum physics. At the subatomic level, the outcome of certain events would seem not to be determined by definite laws. Why does *A* happen, not *B*? One answer, proposed by physicist Hugh Everett, is that *both* things happen, but in *different* "*worlds*." Hence the idea, eagerly taken up by science fiction, of *alternate worlds*, one for each possible outcome. Lewis seems to be entertaining a similar possibility, but from a different, more radical angle: What if, he argues, all the things that *might* have been (*counterfactuals*, as philosophers call them), are actually true *in some other world*? There is a world where Japan won World War II, or JFK was not assassinated, or even where pigs fly—for such a world may not just contain different possible facts, but different physical laws. If such worlds are possible, then what's to stop them existing too? Nothing, says Lewis. Therefore, in some way, they must.

Are zombies possible? They're not
just possible; they're actual. We're
all zombies. Nobody is conscious.

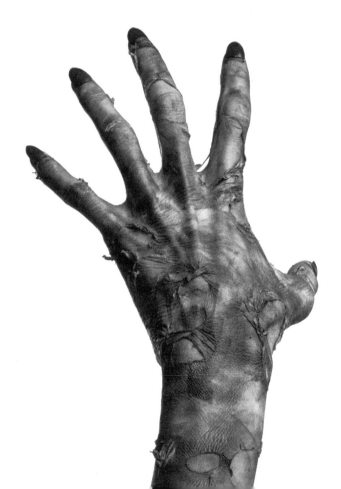

96

DANIEL DENNETT
b. 1942

SOURCE: *Consciousness Explained*
DATE: 1991
FIELD: Philosophy of mind

I assume that I possess a single self or "I." If pressed, I might say that "I" reside in my head, looking out through my eyes. The problem with this view is that, while not in itself a scientific theory, it does seem to lead to scientific and philosophical misconceptions. For instance, Descartes assumed that "I," my thinking self, is the *true* self, a ghostly entity piloting the body from its control room in the brain, where it reviews live or recorded "footage" from the day's activities on internal "screens" (the imagination).

However, this "Cartesian theater," as American philosopher Daniel Dennett calls it, is false; the "I" is actually an illusion, built up through various neurological processes, and is like a sort of story that we tell ourselves. "Reality" isn't as seamless nor as objective as we think, but something constructed, filled out and patched up—as are we.

As noted previously, philosophers such as Nagel have pointed out that perceptions are tinged by indefinable qualities or "qualia": the smell of coffee, the redness of a rose. Qualia therefore seem to present a problem for certain types of *physicalism*: If the mind is just a physical thing—the brain—then where do qualia reside? It seems odd to say that "redness" is merely a pattern of neurons. To which Dennett's answer is: *not* if qualia don't actually exist. We behave as if we have such states, even convince ourselves that we do, but it's all illusion. In truth, there's no "I," and no subjective experience; in this sense, we're just high-functioning "zombies."

One is a person because
of what he is, not because
of what he acquires.

97

KWAME GYEKYE
b. 1939

SOURCE: "Person and Community" in *Person and Community: Ghanaian Philosophical Studies 1*, Gyekye & Wiredu (eds.)
DATE: 1992
FIELD: Philosophy of mind

What is a person? Is it something we are, or something we (or at least some of us) achieve? Are there degrees of it? The issue of "personhood" is a central question in modern philosophy, and there are different responses to it. Here, Ghanaian philosopher Kwame Gyekye argues that the capacity to be a person is inherent, and therefore cannot be taken away.

To understand Gyekye's position, perhaps it is best to consider the view that he is opposing. As individuals grow up, they generally acquire more status—through learning and education; through change in family roles and increased social responsibilities; through work, property, and possessions. In this sense, people who have achieved greater social status are more fully "persons" than those who have not: A baby has less responsibility, education, etc, than an average adult, and accordingly is less of a person.

While acknowledging that individuals need communities in order to survive and flourish, Gyekye nonetheless denies that personhood is dependent on community. We are persons *before* we achieve any sort of social status, and a lack of social success or influence cannot limit or take that away from us. What jobs we have, what things we own, our character traits or physical attributes, Gyekye considers to be accidental features. Being a person requires only that we possess an *okra* ("soul"), and as such, he believes, we deserve respect, and possess rights, merely by virtue of being human. How we fare in the game of life is irrelevant.

PROPAGANDA IS
TO A DEMOCRACY
WHAT THE
BLUDGEON IS TO A
TOTALITARIAN STATE.

98

NOAM CHOMSKY
b. 1928

SOURCE: Radio interview, WBAI, New York
DATE: 1992
FIELD: Political philosophy

We tend to think of propaganda as something used against enemy states, or by totalitarian regimes to control their citizens. As such, it implies deliberate manipulation of opinion through disinformation, distortion, and lies. This assertion, made by American political commentator and linguist Noam Chomsky, is therefore shocking, as the cornerstone of a democracy would seem to be freedom of the press from bias and coercion. Yet Chomsky's point is that while an authoritarian state might directly censor the "news," even perhaps resorting to violence and intimidation, a democratic state employs less obvious methods of control.

In *Manufacturing Consent*, with American media analyst Edward S. Herman, Chomsky lays out the "propaganda model" of the media, whereby the various power structures within a society—the government, the dominant forms of industry, the banks and institutions—act as "filters" for the news by exerting subtle forms of pressure. For instance, most news organizations rely heavily on advertising. Yet a newspaper that printed stories criticizing certain business practices, or called for restrictions on trade, might find its advertisers dropping out. A journalist who failed to adopt a particular line might find himself cut off from vital governmental sources of statistics and information. And so, by these and other indirect means, a democratic nation's media finds itself shaped to reflect the underlying values of those in power.

Of course, this doesn't mean there's no difference of opinion. In fact, the "better"-quality newspapers will often give voice to competing views. Yet overall, as a percentage of coverage, the dominant message will always reinforce a narrow spectrum of political opinion.

You ask a philosopher a question and, after he or she has talked for a bit, you don't understand your question anymore.

99

PHILIPPA FOOT
1920–2010

SOURCE: Quoted in *Philosophers* by Steve Pyke
DATE: 1993
FIELD: General

Asked along with other fellow professionals to characterize philosophy, the response of English philosopher Philippa Foot seems to capture the experience of many on coming to the subject for the first time, while also echoing Plato's contention that philosophy begins in wonder. Curious about something, we start to question; but, in philosophy, such questions lead us not to conclusive answers, but only to further questions, until, farther and farther from our original starting point, we may look up to realize that we don't know how we got here, or even where "here" is!

Underlying this picture is the idea that philosophy is a search for ultimate answers. Like the child who infuriatingly responds to its parent's responses with another "Why?", the philosopher's curiosity can seem perverse, even pointless: What if there *are* no ultimate answers? Yet there may be a reason for *that*, too—that humans are not capable of understanding certain things, perhaps, or that the world *just is* a certain way. This knowledge of our limits is also a certain sort of wisdom.

Unlike science, philosophy is not generally a tool for useful discoveries, and it's rarely able to prove anything. And if it is a tool, then it's one that the philosopher is as likely to turn upon himself, using it to question his own trustworthiness, perceptions, or motives. This ceaseless doubting and questioning may seem exhausting, and it can be, but it is not a purely negative activity, for it is a practice that will (hopefully) result in deeper understanding of…what were we talking about?

Knowledge is no guarantee of good behavior, but

ignorance is a virtual guarantee of bad behavior.

100

MARTHA NUSSBAUM
b. 1947

SOURCE: *Not For Profit: Why Democracy Needs the Humanities*
DATE: 2010
FIELD: Ethics

Plato had thought that wrongdoing was a matter of ignorance; no one *knowingly* did wrong. In contrast, his pupil Aristotle thought that there were occasions where, although we know what the right thing to do is, we fail to follow it. Why is this? It is basically a matter of weakness of will—what Aristotle termed *akrasia*—where our reason is overwhelmed by irrational impulse (desire, pleasure, satisfaction of short-term goals).

Siding with Aristotle, American philosopher Martha Nussbaum acknowledges that merely teaching people right from wrong is no guarantee that they will act morally. However, this makes ethical and emotional education all the more important. Nussbaum argues that modern trends in education have emphasized "useful" subjects—math, science, engineering, computing—at the expense of the humanities. What good is Shakespeare in the jobs market? Will knowing about Kant's categorical imperative help put food on the table? Yet while (according to some measures) such knowledge provides little tangible, practical benefit, we turn our back on it at our peril, for a rounded education in philosophy, literature, and the arts is important in developing a free-thinking, emotionally mature human being; not just a cog in the economic machine, but a fully developed individual, ready to play their part as a citizen.

It is an argument that Aristotle himself would have had sympathy with; we are most fully human when we are fully involved in cultural, political, and social life. As business and technology throw up ever greater ethical issues—climate change, genetic engineering, Internet privacy—we need such citizens now more than ever.

INDEX